Competency-Based Interviews

REVISED EDITION

Competency-Based INTERVIEWS

How to Master the Tough Interview Style Used by the Fortune 500s

Robin Kessler

CAREER PRESS
Pompton Plains, NJ

Competency-Based Interviews, Revised Edition
Typeset by Eileen Munson
Cover design by Jeff Piasky
Printed in the U.S.A.

To order this title, please call toll-free 1-800-CAREER-1 (NJ and Canada: 201-848-0310) to order using VISA or MasterCard, or for further information on books from Career Press.

The Career Press, Inc.
220 West Parkway, Unit 12
Pompton Plains, NJ 07444
www.careerpress.com

Library of Congress Cataloging-in-Publication Data

Kessler, Robin, 1955-
Competency-based interviews : how to master the tough interview style used by the Fortune 500s / by Robin Kessler. --
Rev. ed.
p. cm.
Rev. ed. of: Competency-based interviews. c2006.
Includes bibliographical references and index.
ISBN 978-1-60163-221-0 -- ISBN 978-1-60163-594-5 (ebook) 1. Employment interviewing. 2. Core competencies. 3. Self-presentation. I. Title.

HF5549.5.I6K47 2012
650.14′4--dc23

2012013332

This is for my mother,
with love and thanks.

Acknowledgments

As always, a huge thank you to everyone who helped with this book. I would, however, like to give a few people some special recognition.

To Paula Hanson: Thank you for doing the initial editing and providing advice when I came up against problems. Any kind of problem. And for hanging in as a good friend for a very long time.

To Steven Lait, graphic artist for Costco and the former editorial cartoonist for the *Oakland Tribune* and ANG Group, who drew the cartoons for this book: Thank you for doing great work and being the best editorial cartoonist on the planet—as well as one of my favorite cousins.

I'd like to thank the consultants Ed Cripe, Cybelle Lyon, Cara Capretta Raymond, Michael Friedman, Dr. Kay Lillig Cotter, and Ken Abosch for sharing your expertise, time, opinions, and personal competencies. Having the opportunity to talk with each of you helped me make this book considerably stronger.

To David Heath, Dessie Nash, Blake Nolingberg, Mindy Wertheimer, Erica Graham, Chip Smith, Kalen Phillips, Stephen Sye, Diane Schad Dayhoff, Mary Alice Eureste, and Bill Baumgardt: Thank you for being subject-matter experts in your professional areas and answering all my questions for the book.

To Ron Fry, Michael Pye, Adam Schwartz, Kirsten Dalley, Laurie Kelly-Pye, and the rest of the staff at Career Press: Thank you for doing a great job of making my words look good, the book look better, and being great to work with.

To my other friends and relatives: Thank you once again for putting up with my leaving early, not calling as often, and not being as available to go out to dinner, the movies, or anything else. Since this book is now finished, please call me.

Contents

Introduction		9
Chapter 1:	Understand Competency-Based Interview Systems	19
Chapter 2:	Identify Key Competencies	29
Chapter 3:	Know What Interviewers Are Trained to Look For	41
Chapter 4:	Expect Competency-Based Behavioral Questions	51
Chapter 5:	Prove Competencies With Examples	59
Chapter 6:	Present Yourself as a Strong Candidate	69
Chapter 7:	Consider Other Important Interview Tips	79
	Mid-Book Review 89	
Chapter 8:	Look at Case Studies for Ideas to Make Your Interviewing Stronger	101
Chapter 9:	Understand How a Typical Competency-Based Interview Flows	115
Chapter 10:	Learn From Other Interviewees	123
Chapter 11:	Stay Current With Interview Technology and Practices	137
Chapter 12:	Develop Global Competencies for the Future	151

Chapter 13: Send a Thank-You Note, Follow Up, Get the Offer, and Negotiate 163

Chapter 14: Actively Manage Your Career in Competency-Based Organizations 171

Chapter 15: Use Competency-Based Resumes to Get Your Next Interview 179

Chapter 16: Think Long-Term and Make Change Work for You 189

Appendix A: List of Core Competencies 193

Appendix B: Competencies for Case Studies 205

Appendix C: Examples of Illegal Interview Questions 211

Notes 213

Bibliography 215

Index 217

About the Author 223

Introduction

What can you do today to be a star at interviewing and improve your career? How can you get the offer you want from the organization you want to work for? How can you move forward in your career?

The first step is to think strategically. Why do publishers choose to offer on certain book proposals and not others? Why do certain products do especially well and others don't? How did Oprah become a star, and what does she do to make sure she stays a star? How can she be so good at interviewing, acting, and developing and publishing her magazine? What made Nelson Mandela from South Africa and Aung San Suu Kyi from Myanmar so admired worldwide that they both won Nobel Peace Prizes? Why did you—or someone you know—get into a prestigious college? Why do certain people get selected for the best assignments and the best jobs, and what causes other qualified candidates to be rejected?

The answers to these questions are complex, but if you really think about it, there are three basic steps you need to take to improve your ability to get what you want.

What It Takes to Win

1. Learning what it takes to win is the first step.
2. Doing the things that it takes to win is the second step.
3. Recognizing that what it takes to win can change—sometimes rapidly—is the third step.

The more quickly you identify how things are changing and adjust your approach, the more quickly you will be successful. Realistically, we need to expect changes. New tools, new approaches, and new strategies can cause decision-makers to make different decisions. If we adapt to these changes earlier than others, we increase our probability of winning. That's all. Oprah may have strong artistic abilities, and Nelson Mandela and Aung San Suu Kyi have demonstrated exceptional political skills. All three are obviously more intelligent than the average person, both intellectually and emotionally. But they have also overcome major life challenges. Oprah has dealt with child abuse, Nelson Mandela was imprisoned for 27 years, and Aung San Suu Kyi was released in 2011 after 15 years of house arrest. Clearly, all three figured out what it took to get ahead in their fields, and have mastered staying ahead of the game as their environments changed. Mandela went on to become the president of South Africa from 1994–1999, and as of this writing, Aung San Suu Kyi is running for parliament in Myanmar (formerly known as Burma).

One of the key abilities that will help you manage your career is learning how to interview more effectively and convince the interviewer that you are the best candidate for the job. Interviewing well is critical if you want to be successful. So how can you take the three steps that it takes to win and apply them to interviewing? This book will show you how to be more successful by:

- ★ Teaching you how to recognize the changes in interviewing that are being implemented at most sophisticated organizations.
- ★ Explaining what today's interviewers are looking for.
- ★ Showing you how to emphasize how your competencies match the employer's needs.
- ★ Developing a plan to ensure you perform well in every critical interview.

When systems change and grow, we need to be smarter than our competitors and recognize those changes as early as possible, the way Oprah and these Nobel Peace Prize winners have. If we aren't aware, our own careers may be negatively affected. We need time to develop and adjust our strategy, because employers do periodically change the systems they use to select employees. If we don't change our approach, we will eventually become less valuable to our current employer, as well. We all need to take responsibility for actively managing our career, and that includes changing our strategy to respond to the changes introduced by higher-ups. As we become increasingly astute, we may be able to anticipate some of these changes and prepare for them.

This book will give you a new—and better—strategy to interview more effectively and improve your ability to get the job you want. If you use this approach you will increase your chances of:

- ⋆ Being selected for the most competitive positions.
- ⋆ Winning the best job at a new organization.
- ⋆ Getting a great first job or internship.
- ⋆ Being chosen for that critical promotion in your current organization.
- ⋆ Taking control of your career path.
- ⋆ Increasing your salary.
- ⋆ Obtaining more satisfying assignments and more challenging work.

What's Different?

Understanding exactly *how* human resources managers, line managers, and professionals approach interviewing and hiring has always given candidates an advantage in the interview process. If you know what the interviewer is looking for—and you're savvy enough to know how to use that information—you'll have an edge in the interview. More than half of the Fortune 500 companies and other major organizations all around the world are now using competency-based systems to help select and manage employees. Here are just a few examples: American Express, Johnson & Johnson, Coca-Cola, Toyota, Bank of America, BP, Wells Fargo, General Motors, HP, Radio Shack, HCA, Carlson Companies, BHP, IBM, General Electric, PDVSA, Anheuser-Busch, Girl Scouts USA, the U.S. Federal Reserve System, and the province of British Columbia in Canada. Some of these organizations have worked with competency-based systems for more than 20 years, and they are becoming increasingly sophisticated in how they are applying them. Other companies, government agencies, and nonprofit organizations have adopted competencies more recently or are looking at the possibility of using them in the near future. Competency-based systems help organizations manage their human resources, everything from selecting employees to evaluating, training, paying, and promoting them.

Competency-based interviews and competency-based appraisals are the two most common ways companies are using competencies to help improve the caliber of their employees. More and more companies are including a list of competencies they need in ads on their own Websites and on Websites such as Monster.com and Careerbuilder.com. Since

January 2003, when I first saw the need for my book *Competency-Based Resumes*, the number of job advertisements that specifically list the competencies the employer is looking for continues to increase significantly every time I check.

In early March of 2012, Monster.com ran advertisements asking for competencies from organizations of all sizes. Companies with competency-based job advertisements shown that day included:

- IBM
- Google
- Lockheed Martin
- Prudential
- KPMG
- Sanofi
- Konica Minolta
- Invensys
- Expedia
- Massachusetts General Hospital
- Ingersoll-Rand
- Luminant
- ConAgra

CareerBuilder ads specifically mentioning competencies around the same time included:

- DuPont
- General Mills
- Schlumberger
- Grainger

Employees at the best competency-based employers now have the ability to look up information about critical competencies on their employer's Website or in employee handbooks or manuals, which are now usually available online. The competencies for their current positions are almost always covered as part of their appraisal.

What Are Competencies?

Paul Green, in his book *Building Robust Competencies* (Jossey-Bass, 1999), defines an individual competency as "a written description of measurable work habits and personal skills used to achieve a work objective." Some organizations define competencies slightly differently as "underlying characteristics, behavior, knowledge, and skills required to differentiate performance." They define what superior performers do more often, in more situations, and with better results. Put simply, competencies are the key characteristics of the most successful performers that help them be so successful. Organizations benefit from working with competencies because it gives them a more effective and more sophisticated way to manage, measure, and improve the quality of their employees. Not surprisingly, the use of competencies is continuing to grow. According to Signe Spencer, a senior consultant with the Hay Group in Boston and the coauthor of *Competence at Work* (John Wiley & Sons, 1993), "In the last 15 years, we have seen an explosion of interest in competency work at all levels worldwide." Competencies are not just a trend!

Competencies that are relevant for all positions organization-wide are called **core competencies**. Competencies used in interviewing and other applications may be identified at the departmental or functional level, or even at the individual level. Being successful as an accountant will require different competencies than those required for a sales position. In Chapter 2, I will spend more time explaining competencies and giving you the information you need to successfully identify the relevant competencies for the position you want, *before* the interview. Many organizations choose not to use the term *competencies*. They prefer to use other terms, such as *success factors*, *attributes*, *values*, *dimensions*, and so on. Each of these terms means something slightly different, and decision-makers have good reasons for choosing them. For candidates, though, it simply makes sense to look at all of these categories for information describing what the employer is really looking for—those key characteristics or competencies. Competency-based systems designed by consultants and corporations can be complex. This book will help you understand these systems and give you the tools you need as a candidate to navigate your way through them.

What Are Competency-Based Interviews?

Today, more and more interviewers at the best companies are using behavioral interviewing techniques to help determine how competent candidates are in the key areas most critical for success. Behavioral interviewing has been in use for more than 20 years in most sophisticated organizations, but behavioral interview questions *targeting relevant competencies* have only been in use in the last 10 to 15 years. Interviewers at many of the best organizations are being trained to use these new competency-based systems and evaluate candidates in a much more complex and comprehensive way than they did in the past. They are now taught to evaluate the candidate's fit for the position based on his or her perceived competency level, and assess the candidate's nonverbal and verbal communication in a more sophisticated way. Organizations may use different names (including *targeted selection interviewing* and *evidence-based interviewing*) to describe what is essentially competency-based interviewing. One approach to competency-based interviewing involves asking primary questions targeting each key competency. Another approach asks interviewers to identify evidence of competencies by listening closely to the answers to questions and follow-up questions (also called *probes*). In Chapter 1, we'll be looking at both of these approaches in more detail.

Despite all of these changes, most career counselors and candidates haven't updated their approach to interviewing, resumes, and other job-search techniques to include the competencies employers are now looking for. Instead, they are marketing candidate strengths and accomplishments the same way they always have. It's time to accept that the job market has changed and adapt our approach accordingly. Competencies are becoming the way the most respected organizations measure whether to interview and hire candidates. For candidates trying to turn their interview into a job offer, it's time to change and be more strategic. It's time to learn how to use your competencies to convince employers you are the best candidate—because you can prove to them you have the critical competencies they need.

As the saying goes, you don't want to be fighting today's war using equipment, strategy, and tactics from the last century.

It's up to you to learn how to interview the competency-based way. To do this, you need to:

1. Understand competency-based interview systems.
2. Identify the key competencies for the position.
3. Know what interviewers are trained to look for.
4. Expect competency-based behavioral questions.
5. Prove your competencies with examples.
6. Present yourself as a strong candidate.
7. Consider other important interview tips.
8. Make sure you are ready for the interview.
9. Look at case studies for ideas to make your interviewing stronger.
10. Understand how a typical competency-based interview unfolds.
11. Learn from other interviewees.
12. Realize competency-based interviewing is becoming the international standard.

13. Stay current with interview technology and practices.
14. Send a thank-you note, follow up, get an offer, and negotiate.

Once you get that great new job, eventually you may need to learn how to conduct competency-based interviews, too. And you will be more successful in your new position if you take the time to follow the suggestions in the final chapter on managing your career in a competency-based organization. By following the suggestions in this book, you will perform better in any interview and increase the probability of an offer. Learning to master the competency-based interview will also make you a better communicator in meetings, in one-on-one interactions, in presentations, and in other types of interviews.

Organizations also benefit when their candidates learn how to interview more effectively. If more people gave well-thought-out answers that illustrate their experience with competencies, interviewers would be able to make more informed hiring decisions. They would have the information they needed to truly hire the most competent person for the job. Even strong, highly competent candidates can benefit from interview coaching or training to help them think about their *best* accomplishments before an interview. Even though most managers know that the best employees aren't always the best interviewees, they usually still make the decision based on the interview.

Are you ready to start sharpening your interviewing skills so the interviewer will realize you are the most competent candidate? Let's get started!

★

Note: Unless stated otherwise, all direct quotes in this book were derived from interviews with the person or persons quoted.

Key Points for the Introduction

An individual competency is a written description of measurable work habits and personal skills used to achieve a work objective.

Key Questions	Answers
What does it take to win in today's organizations?	1. Learning what it takes to win. 2. Doing the things it takes to win. 3. Recognizing that what it takes to win often changes—sometimes rapidly.

Key Questions	Answers
How can I increase my chances of getting the position I want?	Competency-based organizations rely on a different system for evaluating and measuring success, particularly when selecting, promoting, and training their employees. Understanding how competency-based systems work is vital to success in today's organizations. The most important thing to remember is that these systems always change. You need to adjust your own approach to match the employer's changes.
What are competencies?	The key characteristics that the most successful employees have that help them be so successful.
What are core competencies?	Core competencies are used organization-wide to help achieve organizational objectives or goals.
What are the other levels of competencies?	◆ Departmental or functional. ◆ Individual.
What are the two most common competency-based applications?	◆ Competency-based appraisals. ◆ Competency-based selection processes, including interviewing.
What are behavioral interview questions?	Interviewers ask questions to assess how competent candidates are in several areas. Behavioral interviewing is based on the theory that past behavior is the best predictor of future behavior. In other words, *past success predicts future success.*
What can you do to excel in interviews for competitive positions?	Your answers to interview questions must be focused (focused on the competencies desired), powerful (use powerful words to describe your competency), and concise (make a point, make it clear, and use precise wording).
How can you keep promoting your competencies after you are hired?	Strategic marketing tools include competency-based resumes, effective cover letters, networking, and polished interview skills. Focus on the competencies required by your current employer if you want to be considered for promotions or other opportunities.

Key Questions	Answers
How are companies using competencies to strengthen their workforce?	They are using competencies to: ◆ Advertise for candidates. ◆ Screen candidate resumes. ◆ Interview, using behavioral techniques. ◆ Select employees. ◆ Evaluate employees. ◆ Train employees. ◆ Promote employees. ◆ Reward employees. ◆ Determine assignments.

Chapter 1

Understand Competency-Based Interview Systems

When we were students most of us realized the importance of understanding what the teacher or professor was looking for—which assignments were required and which were optional. If we are playing sports, we need to understand the strengths, vulnerabilities, and game plan of our opponent, even if we are the number-one seed in the tournament. When we give a business presentation, we need to understand the needs and interests of the audience before we start developing the speech. Figuring out what other people are expecting is critical to success in most if not all aspects of life. In an interview, we simply have to convince them that we will fit well in the organization and have the skills needed to do the job.

Before you start preparing for an interview, it is important to understand the method of interviewing that will be used by the interviewer. Some organizations are still fairly traditional in their approach to interviewing. Many hiring managers still make decisions about candidates based simply on whether or not they *like* them. In addition, they may focus on whether the candidate meets their basic requirement on credentials, such as grades and class standing. Many law firms and more traditional companies are still interviewing candidates this way. Some hiring managers use hypothetical questions that ask what a candidate would do in a given scenario. People who like this interview style believe it gives them a chance to see how candidates think on their feet, but many others believe that it is not as effective as finding out how individuals have performed in the past. This type of interview, which has been used by consulting firms for years, includes questions based on hypothetical and real cases, and can be used to assess a candidate's ability to answer difficult case-study questions under pressure while the interviewer assesses his or her strengths in key competency areas. (See Chapter 13 for details on case-study interviews.) That said, most organizations with good reputations have realized that the old-style interviews aren't terribly effective in helping them choose employees. They've changed to the newer, competency-based interview style because they believe in staying current. According to Dr. Amy Conn, a senior consultant for assessment solutions at Personnel Decisions, Inc., one of the consulting groups working closely with Fortune 500 companies to develop and improve competency-based systems, "Competency-based interviews are clearly the most widely used approach to an interview." Recognizing how the labor market has changed—and learning how to make those changes work for you—can be the difference between success and failure.

What's Changed?

The most sophisticated employers are primarily using competency-based interview systems to select candidates. If you haven't interviewed recently or if you come from a different culture, you probably know you need some help to do well in the interview. Some candidates think they know what to expect in the interview, and it may take a few bad experiences before they decide their old approach is not working as well as it used to. But even if you are articulate, think well on your feet, have the best credentials, and are confident you are a great candidate, preparing for any interview is important. Remember that how well you perform on the interview gives the interviewers an idea of the quality of work they can expect from you in the future. Whether you are writing a resume, preparing for an interview, or getting ready for a performance review, becoming more aware of what competencies the employer is looking for is the first step toward success. The next step? Learn how to prove to the employer that you are strong in these critical competency areas.

How Does a Competency-Based Interview Work?

Very simply, a competency-based interview is a highly structured interview that involves the use of behavioral questions to help the interviewer assess the candidate based on critical competencies that have already been identified by the employer. Key questions help the interviewer(s) determine how strong candidates are in specific competency areas.

Key Definition

Competency-based interviews are highly structured and use behavioral questions to help the interviewer assess candidates based on critical competencies identified for the position.

Whether you are a candidate who wants to work for an organization using competency-based systems or an employee currently working in a competency-based company, it is important to recognize that it may be time to change your own approach to the process. Retool and retrain. Adjust the sails. Add a warm-up period before running. It's time to accept the fact that in today's most sophisticated organizations, almost all are using competency-based interviews.

The most commonly used competency-based interviewing style involves asking candidates primary questions targeted to the critical competencies for the position. Almost every major consulting firm working to help organizations identify competencies, including Lominger, Personnel Decisions International, Hay Group, and Hewitt Associates, encourages its clients to use structured, competency-based interviewing approach that they have developed. One well-known example of this approach is *targeted selection interviewing*, which was developed by the consulting firm Development Dimensions, Inc. The firm markets targeted selection on its Website by saying it uses behavioral interviewing and helps organizations:

- ★ Identify the competencies needed for all key positions.
- ★ Build interviewing skills and confidence for more accurate selection decisions.
- ★ Increase the efficiency and effectiveness of the employee selection process.

Another approach starts with the manager asking a question about a major accomplishment and then asking follow-up questions to probe for additional information about competencies, strengths, and weaknesses. An example of this approach can be found in Lou Adler's *The One Question Interview*. In both styles, managers are taught to ask candidates behavioral questions, based on the theory that past behavior is the best predictor of future behavior. In other words, past success is the best predictor of future success. The managers are then asked to assess how competent the candidate is in several critical areas. Both interview styles are covered in more detail later in this chapter.

Key Definition

Behavioral questions are based on the theory that past behavior is the best predictor of future behavior.

In order to perform well in a competency-based interview, we need to first understand the two basic interview styles that consider competencies.

Most Typical Approach to Competency-Based Interviews

Example: Johnson & Johnson

Johnson & Johnson has worked with competency-based interviewing for more than 15 years. It has developed interview guides for its senior leaders/executives, for its people, for its individual leaders (professionals and managers), and for campus interviewing. According to Susan Millard, former Vice President for Strategic Talent Management at Johnson & Johnson, "Predicting future success on the job and the competencies that matter the most to performance, and operating with the highest ethical standards are critical to assure we have the talent needed to power our growth and culture at J&J." The company's 2005 recruiting event with 700 MBAs and managers was as successful as it was because interviewers used their updated competency-based Global Leadership Profile Interview Guides and were able to identify some particularly strong candidates. These interview guides review how the interviewer should prepare before the interview, suggest ways to open the interview, ask the interviewer to review the candidate's background and ask questions, and provide several behavioral questions for each critical competency for the position that interviewers can choose from. The interviewer is asked to rate the candidate on competency and communication skills.

Though every competency is very important, I chose to show you the **Results and Performance Driven** example, because it represents one of the most frequently used competencies. Other organizations sometimes use different words to describe the same competency, such as:

- ★ Achieves Results
- ★ Drive for Results
- ★ Performance Bias
- ★ Achieves Goals

<table>
<tr><th colspan="3">Results and Performance Driven</th></tr>
<tr><td>Goal oriented; remains persistent when obstacles are encountered; encourages others to be accountable for their actions; relentlessly focused and committed to customer service; thinks creatively.</td><td colspan="2">Key Examples
☐ Flawless execution—Holds self, direct reports, and others accountable for seamless and compliant execution of tasks and projects.
☐ Accepts stretch goals—Eagerly embraces stretch goals; measures achievements through metrics.
☐ Customer-centric thinking—Makes the customer the center for all decisions to build value; imposes customer focus on others and challenges them to exceed customer expectations.</td></tr>
<tr><td colspan="3">Planned Behavioral Questions
1. Describe an instance when you were particularly effective at achieving results. What steps did you take?
2. Think of a time when you consistently exceeded internal or external customer expectations. How did you do this? What approach did you use?
3. Provide an example of a project or team you managed in which there were many obstacles to overcome. What did you do to address those obstacles?
4. Tell me about a time when you needed to obtain information to better understand a customer. What did you do? How did this information improve your customer service?
5. It is not always easy to achieve required work goals or objectives. Describe a stretch goal or objective that you were able to achieve. Why was this a stretch goal? How did you achieve this goal or objective?</td></tr>
<tr><td>Situation/Task</td><td>Action</td><td>Result</td></tr>
<tr><td></td><td></td><td></td></tr>
</table>

Communication: ______________________________

____

Results and Performance Driven Rating: ☐

(For explanations of the ratings for the previous chart, see Chapter 3.)

Another Approach

Another current approach to interviewing starts with one question and asks the candidate a series of follow-up questions to probe for additional information. This interview technique provides an interesting and different way to assess a candidate by listening for evidence of the candidate's competency (and critical competencies) in his/her answers. The basic technique can be found in this excerpt from an article by consultant Lou Adler, whose firm, Adler Concepts, teaches interviewing skills to major clients. He encourages interviewers to first ask the candidate to think about his or her most significant accomplishment, and then to tell the interviewer about it. Interviewers are then directed to probe for the following information about the accomplishment from the candidate, a process that takes about 15 to 20 minutes:

- ★ A complete description of the accomplishment.
- ★ The company you worked for and what it did.
- ★ The actual results achieved: numbers, facts, changes made, details, amounts.
- ★ When it took place.
- ★ How long it took.
- ★ The importance of this accomplishment to the company.
- ★ Your title and role.
- ★ Why you were chosen.
- ★ The three or four biggest challenges you faced and how you dealt with them.
- ★ A few examples of leadership and initiative.
- ★ Some of the major decisions made.
- ★ The environment and resources available.
- ★ How you made more resources available.
- ★ The technical skills needed to accomplish the objective.
- ★ The technical skills learned and how long it took to learn them.
- ★ The actual role you played.
- ★ The team involved and all of the reporting relationships.
- ★ Some of the biggest mistakes you made.

- ★ How you changed and grew as a person.
- ★ What you would do differently if you could do it again.
- ★ Aspects of the project you truly enjoyed.
- ★ Aspects you didn't especially care for.
- ★ The budget available and your role in preparing it and/or managing it.
- ★ How you did on the project vs. the plan.
- ★ How you developed the plan.
- ★ How you motivated and influenced others, with specific examples to prove your claims.
- ★ How you dealt with conflict, with specific examples.
- ★ Anything else you felt was important to the success of the project.

Adler encourages interviewers to conduct this type of interview because he believes "the insight gained from this type of question would be remarkable. Just about everything you need to know about a person's competency can be extracted from this type of question."[1]

Comparing These Two Types of Interviews

Both types give the interviewers substantive, useful information about candidates. Both ask the interviewers to determine how strong the candidate is in critical competency areas important to be successful in the position. The most common approach looks at several of the most critical competencies and asks the candidate to answer behavioral questions targeting these competencies. The other approach digs deeper into just one or two accomplishments and asks the candidate to look at these accomplishments from different perspectives, including competencies.

So why does all this matter? If you can figure out which type is being used in an interview, you'll be able to give the interviewer better answers. By following the advice in this book, you'll be prepared for both types of interviews—and any variations that may be developed in the future. You need to start thinking about how to prepare for these types of interviews. However, this book will place greater emphasis on helping you to prepare for the first type because it is so much more common.

When you use accomplishments to prove you are strong in each relevant competency during an interview, you can expect follow-up questions to probe how much you know or simply to clarify something that is unclear to the interviewer. It's a good idea to figure out ahead of time how each accomplishment can provide evidence in more than one competency area. As you think about each accomplishment, brainstorm possible follow-up questions you could be asked in order to obtain information about several key competency areas. If you do that, you will be ready for either type of interview. Be smart, be savvy, and figure out what you can expect *before* the interview.

Key Points for Chapter 1

"Competency-based interviews are clearly the most widely used approach to an interview."
—Dr. Amy Conn, Personnel Decisions International

Key Questions	Answers
Is every organization using competency-based interviewing systems?	Most of the more sophisticated organizations worldwide are using competency-based interviewing systems. More traditional companies and law firms are still interviewing and making important decisions based upon the candidate's credentials and whether the interviewer likes the candidate.
How can you tell that you are being given a competency-based interview?	Competency-based interviews are highly structured and use behavioral questions to help the interviewer get good answers from the candidate that help them assess candidates more effectively based on the critical competencies identified for the position.
What is behavioral interviewing?	An interviewing style that is based on the theory that past behavior is the best predictor of future behavior.
How are competency-based interviews structured?	Organizations typically identify three to five primary questions targeting each critical competency area, which interviewers may then use to obtain information from the candidate needed to assess his/her level of competence.

Key Questions	Answers
What is the difference between the two styles of interviewing mentioned in this chapter?	Style #1 is the most widely used type of competency-based interview. Interviewers ask candidates behavioral questions targeting each competency area identified as important for success in the position. Candidates have the opportunity to talk about a larger number of accomplishments. Style #2 asks the candidate to look at one accomplishment and then probes for additional information—including looking at the accomplishment from the perspective of different competencies.

AND HOW DOES A NICELY PREPARED BOWL OF POTPOURRI MAKE JAIL TIME MORE BEARABLE?...
RESUME
MARTHA STEWART
S. Laib

Chapter 2

Identify Key Competencies

I not only use all the brains that I have, but all that I can borrow.

—Woodrow Wilson

I believe in being smart as you can *before* the actual interview. Taking the time to learn what the organization is looking for before the interview is critical if you want to convince the interviewer that you are the best person for the job. If you need to borrow the information from other people, as Woodrow Wilson likely would have done, or by doing online research, take the hint from Nike's ad campaign: *Just do it*. (Nike, by the way, is another company that works with competencies.)

Countries sharing the same language can have different priorities regarding competencies, and within each country different organizations will have different needs—and different competencies. Organizations develop their own lists of competencies and often work closely with consultants to benefit from their expertise in competencies and competency modeling. Conservative companies tend to emphasize very different competencies than more progressive organizations, such as Ben and Jerry's or Starbucks. Think of the difference between United Airlines and Southwest Airlines, for example. Or IBM and Apple. That said, competencies tend to be consistent with the corporate culture that senior managers are trying to create. What is the best way to figure out what the hiring manager will be looking for in the interview? Competencies are a great place to start.

Some organizations list competencies for their positions in their online advertisements. Key competencies (also called success factors, dimensions, and values) may also be part of recruiters' job descriptions. Other organizations may not explicitly list their competencies, but they are still looking for candidates who have the competencies needed to be succesful in those positions. Whether or not a company formally identifies such competencies, however, *all* companies are looking for people who have the competencies needed to be successful in their position.

For example, Boeing listed an opportunity on an industry-specific jobsite called PowerJobsDirect.com in March of 2012 for a human resources general manager position in Vienna, Virginia. They included a list of the competencies required for the position and broke them into categories:

Boeing Leadership Attributes:

[+] Charts the Course
[+] Delivers Results
[+] Finds a Way
[+] Inspires Others
[+] Lives the Boeing Values
[+] Sets High Expectations

General Competencies:

[+] Building Organizational Talent
[+] Customer Focus
[+] Establish Strategic Direction
[+] Managing Conflict

Technical Competencies:

[+] HR Practices/Processes
[+] Influencing Others

When competencies are not explicitly identified, you need to identify them on your own, *before* the interview. The four major steps to identifying a company's competencies are:

1. Think about the obvious competencies for the position.
2. Look at advertisements and postings from competitors.
3. Compile a list of competencies from other sources, including employment Websites, advertisements in newspapers, magazines, and journals, professional associations, and the organization's Website.
4. Select 10 to 15 competencies that would be the most critical for the position you are interested in from Appendix A.

If you already work for an organization and need to interview for a promotion or a new position, you may be able to find the relevant list of competencies for the position:

★ On the company Website.

★ On performance appraisals for employees currently in the position.

- ★ In employee handbooks or other company manuals.
- ★ By asking a colleague or friend working in that department.

One of the main ways you can show how strong a candidate you are is by doing your homework. Take the initiative—be resourceful, and make every effort to find out what the company values most. Even if the organization hasn't stated this explicitly, you can still make an educated guess about the most critical competencies.

When competencies aren't identified, look further.

Step 1: Think About the Obvious Competencies for the Position

In sales, it is critical to focus on results. It doesn't matter how much the managers like you if you don't close the sale. When you don't see the word "competencies" as a heading in an online job posting or advertisement, read further. You may see phrases and words that indicate core, departmental, and individual competencies under headings such as "Required Qualifications," "Job Requirements," or "Required Knowledge, Skills and Abilities." "Leadership Attributes," which was included in the Boeing advertisement, is another way to refer to their leadership competencies.

Step 2: Look at Job Postings on Competitors' Websites

Also check to see if any of the competitors have an equivalent position posted on Monster.com, CareerBuilder.com, or one of the other job sites on the Internet. Then decide whether the same competencies fit the position you are interested in, or whether they need to be reworked for any other reason. (In other words, consider the culture of the organization.) For example, it would be reasonable to assume that the corporate culture at Celestial Seasonings is sufficiently different from the culture at Unilever to cause the competencies that it takes to be successful to be different, as well—even for an equivalent position.

Step 3: Compile a Complete, Thorough List of Competencies for Your Position

There are several ways to develop a broader list of competencies for a particular position. For example, if you are interested in being considered for an IT project manager's position at a company that has not listed competencies in its advertisement, go to:

- An employment Website such as Monster.com or Dice.com, and type in "competencies IT project manager." Look through several of the ads to see if the competencies identified for these positions match what you know about the position at the particular organization you want to work for. (Remember that you do not have to limit this search to your geographic area!)
- Competitors' Websites. Go to the "Careers" section and look at competencies listed in each of their IT project manager positions.
- Employment advertisements for similar positions in newspapers and association publications to see if they have listed competencies.
- Your professional association Website. (For project management, you would want to go to *www.pmi.org* if you live in the United States, to *www.apm.org.uk* in Great Britain, or to an equivalent site for your own country. For human resources, go to *www.shrm.org*.) Look at job listings to see if the organization has identified competencies for the position. Also, check out the research capabilities of the association. Information about key professional competencies may be available online or by calling a research professional on the organization's staff.
- The Website of the organization itself. See if you can find information about the corporate culture to help you identify which competencies are likely to be valued. Information about the organization's mission, vision, or values is often posted online or made available in other organization publications. Read annual reports—particularly those focusing on letters from the chairman and CEO. See if you can figure out what the organization values or where the organization is having problems or feeling pain. Learn more about the organization from other sources. Look for clues indicating the competencies the organization needs now and will need in the future to be successful. Pay particular attention to anything indicating that the organization has changed its competencies, because this may indicate a change in strategy or leadership, or, more simply, a recognition that it was time to update the list to make it more relevant for its employees.

Johnson & Johnson

GLOBAL LEADERSHIP PROFILE

Developing a diverse, robust pipeline of extraordinary leaders

- Integrity and Credo-based Actions ~ lives Credo values; builds trust; tells the truth; initiates transparency into problems; demonstrates genuine caring for people
- Strategic Thinking ~ driven to envision a better future; takes any role or job and makes it better; has relentless dissatisfaction with status quo; motivated to leave things better than they were; a change agent
- Big Picture Orientation with Attention to Detail ~ able to operate in two "worlds" simultaneously e.g., growth and cost control, enterprise and operating company success; sees the why as well as the what; can zoom in or out as needed
- Organization & Talent Development ~ motivates and empowers others to achieve a desired action; enjoys developing a diverse group of people; champions diversity; instills confidence; attracts good people; demonstrates a track record of people development; brings out the best in others; net exporter of successful talent; invests time to be personally "connected" with the organization
- Intellectual Curiosity ~ sees the possibilities; willing to experiment; cultivates new ideas; comfortable with ambiguity and uncertainty
- Collaboration and Teaming ~ puts interests of enterprise above own; works well across functions and groups; builds teams effectively; inspires followership; instills a global mindset; champions best practices
- Sense of Urgency ~ proactively senses and responds to problems and opportunities; works to reduce "cycle" time; takes action when needed
- Prudent Risk-taking ~ inner confidence to take risks and learn from experience; courage to grab opportunities or shed non-viable businesses; willing to make tough calls
- Self-awareness and Adaptability ~ resilient; has personal modesty and humility; willing to learn from others; patient, optimistic, flexible and adaptable
- Results and Performance Driven ~ assumes personal ownership and accountability for business results and solutions; consistently delivers results that meet or exceed expectations; makes the customer central to all thinking; keeps the focus on driving customer value

v2. 02/08/06

Key Point

The approach used in this book is different from traditional approaches to preparing for an interview. The competency-based interview approach, as with the competency-based resume approach, *always* looks at the employer's needs first. Only then are you encouraged to think about how you fit what the employer is looking for—the critical competencies the employer needs—to be successful now and in the future.

Analyze online and traditional advertisements and job postings, and focus on words that might be on an organization's list of competencies organization-wide or for a particular position. Remember that most of the competencies can be stated several ways, as most words have synonyms.

One way to help yourself think about this is to simply ask the question, "What competencies would I look for if *I* were the hiring manager?"

Identify the most relevant competencies for a specific position by starting with core, departmental/functional, or individual competencies that you have already identified for your professional area or industry. Most organizations typically identify between eight and 12 of the most critical competencies for most positions to make it easier for managers and employees to track and evaluate the information, although this number may depend on which consulting firm the organization worked with to develop its list. In late 2011, I had the chance to do competency-based interview training at a European-based engineering firm, as well as a "lunch and learn" program for an affinity group at a refinery owned by a major international oil company. I noticed that both groups had just a few major competencies each, with a more detailed list of competencies grouped underneath them. This was especially obvious at the oil company because I had done several presentations there after the first edition of this book came out in 2006, and so I knew know their list had changed. I spoke to two consultants who confirmed that they, too, had noticed this trend toward using fewer major competencies in the last few years.

Also spend a few minutes thinking about the level of expertise in each competency needed to be successful in the position, and what kind of experience you can mention to prove you have that competency *at the applicable level*. Interviewers will be evaluating how much expertise you have in each of the organization's core competencies. For example, you could be a person with a great deal of integrity, but not very good at seeking out information.

According to Signe Spencer of the Hay Group, the 10 most common competencies being used by organizations today are:

1. Achievement/Results Orientation
2. Initiative
3. Impact and Influence
4. Customer Service Orientation
5. Interpersonal Understanding
6. Organizational Awareness
7. Analytical Thinking
8. Conceptual Thinking
9. Information Seeking
10. Integrity

These competencies are not listed by rank order. They are simply the 10 most common.

When an organization's needs change, the competencies it values the most will change, too. Consider how radically different the Federal Emergency Management Agency's needs were the week before and the week after Hurricane Katrina hit Louisiana and the Mississippi Gulf Coast in late August of 2005. Dealing with an unprecedented major crisis can cause needs and requirements to change in almost an instant. Most of us watching the response saw that government agencies at the federal, state, and local levels did not respond well. They were not successful in how they handled the crisis because they were unable or unwilling to reprioritize their core competencies quickly enough. Likewise, let's say a new CEO decides to change the strategy of the company from being the lowest-cost producer to the highest-quality producer. The technical and business competencies needed and valued by the company can and should change to make the new strategy successful. Or, let's say a consulting firm or a law firm obtains a major new client that insists on better customer service than the firm is used to providing. Suddenly, the entire firm must learn the latest customer service information, and evidence of strong customer service may now help employees get on the fast track to promotion or partnership.

Despite the fact that organizations often prioritize their competencies differently at different times, most still value and use most of the 10 standard competencies listed previously. When we look at each competency, however, it is important to remember that varying degrees of knowledge, skills, and abilities will be needed in order for the candidate to be successful, depending on the level of the position. For example, we would expect a senior vice president of human resources at a major company to be much stronger in Organizational Awareness (which is another way of saying political savvy) than a recent college graduate just starting out in human resources.

Organizations typically identify three to five competency levels and use different terms to describe those levels. At Penn State University, for example, the levels are baseline, intermediate, proficient, advanced, and mastery.[1] Senior-level managers can be rated as advanced (or the equivalent) in some competencies, intermediate or proficient in others, and receive the mastery rating in only one area, if at all. Some organizations choose to recognize these level-based differences by weighting the competencies one way for a junior level professional and another way for managers in the same functional area. The example in the following box shows you the way one competency—Planning and Organizing—can be weighted differently for a supervisor, a middle manager, and a senior manager.

Competency Levels: Planning and Organizing

Competency definition: The ability to visualize a sequence of actions needed to achieve a goal and to estimate the resources required. A preference for acting in a structured, thorough manner.

Individual Contributors to Supervisors:

- Manage own time and personal activities.
- Break complex activities into manageable tasks.
- Identify possible obstacles to planned achievement.

Middle Managers:

- Produce contingency plans for possible future occurrences.
- Estimate in advance the resources and time scales needed to meet objectives.
- Coordinate team activities to make the best use of individual skills and specialties.

Senior Managers:

- Identify long-term operational implications of business plans.
- Effectively plan utilization of all resources.[2]

Because competencies are often prioritized differently from organization to organization, and because functions and departments within organizations may have different needs, a more complete list of competencies is included in Appendix A.

Step 4: Select the Most Critical Competencies for the Position

Read through the competencies included in Appendix A very carefully. Mark the ones that are most applicable or most heavily weighted for the position you are interested in. Then go back and edit the list to choose the competencies that you think the hiring manager would select. Identify the 10 to 20 most important. Next, decide whether there will be any functional/departmental or individual position competencies that you think the hiring manager might put on the list. For example, if you are interested in a sales position, is there a possibility that, in addition to achieving results, territory management might be critical for success? Do you think the engineering manager hiring a chemical engineer for a plant might be interested in a candidate's knowledge of statistical process control?

Because most organizations usually identify between eight and 12 competencies for each position, sometimes fewer, my suggestion is to identify 10 to 15 competencies. This will improve your chances of including the competencies the organization has selected. Look through the list and think about how important each competency is in being successful in the position. Because many organizations weight the competencies based upon importance, it is worth spending some time to consider which competencies deserve the most emphasis. While recognizing that organizations may define different levels of expertise for each competency, I believe that the best way to write a competency-based resume or to prepare for a competency-based interview is to (1) identify the most critical competencies for the position, and (2) think about how to present your accomplishments in such as way that they prove that you have a high level of experience in each of these key competency areas. Once you've put together a good list of competencies for the particular position you want, keep on improving the list, either through research or by asking your networking contacts.

Great work! You've completed the first major part of getting ready for a competency-based interview. Now we are ready to begin working on the next step to help you succeed in a competency-based interview.

Key Points for Chapter 2

The competency-based approach always looks at the employer's needs first.

Key Questions	Answers
What are the first steps in identifying the *right* competencies to help you prepare for a competency-based interview?	◆ Think first about the obvious competencies for the position. ◆ Look at the advertisement, posting, or job description from the organization.
What resources can help employees identify competencies for interviews within their organization?	◆ The organization's Website. ◆ Performance appraisals for the position. ◆ Employee handbooks and other internal organization manuals. ◆ Colleagues working in the relevant department or in the position itself.
If the organization doesn't provide a list of the competencies it is looking for, how do you get started compiling your own list of key competencies? Where can you find clues as to what these competencies could be?	◆ Think about what competencies would be obvious for the position. ◆ Look at advertisements and postings for equivalent positions with competitors. Try to determine if the competencies they list will work for the position you are interested in. ◆ Visit employment Websites such as Monster.com or Dice.com and look at equivalent jobs for competency lists. ◆ Look at competitors' Websites. ◆ Read through your professional association Website thoroughly. ◆ Look at employment advertisements in newspapers, association publications, and other sources. ◆ Go to the Website of the target organization and read through its publications to find information about its culture and values.

Key Questions	Key Answers
What are some of the most standard competencies used by organizations?	1. Achievement/Results Orientation 2. Initiative 3. Impact and Influence 4. Customer Service Orientation 5. Interpersonal Understanding 6. Organizational Awareness 7. Analytical Thinking 8. Conceptual Thinking 9. Informational Seeking 10. Integrity Remember, these are the most standard and are by no means the only competencies that may be desired by the target organization. Each organization develops its own list of competencies, and the list can differ based on the goals and overall culture of the organization.

Never ascribe to malice that which can be adequately explained by incompetence.

—Napoleon Bonaparte

S. Laib
SO I GUESS YOU'RE READY TO BEGIN THE INTERVIEW, MR. CRUISE?....
RESUME
TOM CRUISE

Chapter 3

Know What Interviewers Are Trained to Look For

You got to be careful if you don't know where you're going, because you might not get there.

—Yogi Berra

To add a new interpretation to Yogi Berra's point, if you don't know what to expect in your job search, you are unlikely to do well in the interview or receive an offer. This chapter will give you some ideas about what interviewers in the best companies are trained to look for today. Knowing what interviewers want can give you a significant edge as long as you are smart enough to use the information the right way. Always consider the organization's needs first; then, figure out whether and to what extent you match those needs. Before the interview, you need to think about how you can back up your assertions—*with evidence*—that you are competent in the areas the organization needs to be successful.

First we'll cover some of the basics included in interviewer training. What does any interviewer look for in any candidate? What are the types of questions that organizations *don't* want interviewers to ask, because they might lead to lawsuits or discrimination charges? Then we'll talk about how competency-based interviewing builds on these basics to provide interviewers with more structure and a more accurate way of evaluating candidates. The goal of all this training is to help the interviewer determine whether a candidate has the key characteristics—or competencies—that it takes to be successful in a particular job or in an organization.

Aristotle Onassis once said that "the secret to success is to know something nobody else knows." Ultimately you may choose to share some of these secrets of interviewing well with others, or even buy them a copy of this book. That's your decision either way—but I hope you do!

What Have Interviewers Always Been Looking For?

The answer is simple: the best candidate for the job. That hasn't changed. Interviewers are expected to be able to identify strong candidates, offer them a position, and then persuade them to accept the offer. It may help you as a candidate to realize that interviewers only look good when they find someone good enough to get the offer.

Good interviewers *want* you to do well in your interview—their whole job is to hire someone capable. They don't look good to their higher-ups when all they do is eliminate candidates.

Traditionally, most interviewers look for three things:

1. **Can you do the job?** Do you have the right experience and education to do the work? Many interviewers focus their questions in this area. They don't realize that most employees who eventually leave organizations actually have the right background, but may not have the discipline, determination, communication skills, or interpersonal skills to be successful.
2. **Will you do the job?** You may boast a fabulous education and the best technical experience, but what if you're lazy? Discipline, hard work, and determination still count for quite a bit with most interviewers.
3. **How well do you fit with the people, department, organization, and culture?** This is the category that covers your social skills and communication style. You could be an absolute jerk who can't work well with other employees. You may think you are smarter or better than everyone else. You may just have poor communication skills that continually get you into trouble. Or perhaps your personality is just different from those of the other employees in the company. These things matter to managers because most of them have spent more time than they would like dealing with conflicts between employees. Interviewers can make the decision about whether you will be a good fit consciously or unconsciously.

In any interview, the interviewer(s) will be trying to determine whether:

- You have good social skills.
- You are articulate.
- You use good grammar.

- You are dressed appropriately.
- They like you.
- You have the same sense of humor as the rest of the group.
- You handle yourself appropriately.
- Your personality will fit with the people you'll be working with.

More information about the importance of nonverbal communication in the interview process is included in Chapter 6.

How Are Interviewers Taught to Avoid Legal Problems?

Most well-run organizations train their managers, supervisors, and recruiters to avoid asking questions or behaving in ways that can cause legal problems for the organization. Most countries, states, and provinces have employment laws in place to protect their citizens and residents against discrimination. When federal and state laws conflict, most human resources managers will encourage their organizations to comply with the stricter law.

In the United States, federal laws (and many state laws, as well) protect against discrimination based on race, sex, age, religion, disability, veteran status, color, and ethnicity/national origin. Therefore, questions about your marital status, sexual orientation, religious affiliation, illnesses or injuries, where your family is from, or any other type of illegal question should never be asked during an interview. (For examples of illegal questions, please refer to Appendix C.) Interviewers in the United States are trained to focus the interview on what it takes to be successful on the job and away from the candidate's personal life. Good training programs teach interviewers not to ask questions about these "protected" areas unless there is a bona fide occupational reason to do so. An example of a legitimate occupational qualification would be an interviewer selecting a new minister, priest, rabbi, imam, or other religious leader, in which case he or she would be allowed to ask questions about the candidate's religion or religious views. Interviewers at government contractors and subcontractors are trained to give preference to someone who comes from one of the protected classes when candidates are equally qualified. In Europe and many other parts of the world, interviewers are more likely to ask questions about the personal life of a candidate as a way to get to know him or her.

It is still not unheard of for candidates in the United States to tell stories about being asked illegal or inappropriate questions. Why does this still happen? Interviewers may not have been trained on EEO (equal employment opportunity) and diversity or basic interview skills. Or they may simply think that the laws don't matter and they don't have to follow them. Or they may simply be naïve.

If you are ever asked an illegal or inappropriate question, put the question in context. Don't take it personally and don't get angry. Think about what might be the *real* reason or need behind such a question, and see if you can respond to that underlying need in your answer. Always show respect for the interviewer. I can remember during an on-campus interview being asked by a vice president of human resources at a major utility company in the Midwest whether I thought I'd ever get married. I knew the question was illegal, but I put it in context: He had just told me his daughter was in a similar MBA program. I thought that he probably cared a lot more whether his daughter ever married than whether I did. Then I thought about the underlying business need from which the question arose: Would he put energy, effort, and financial resources into training me, only to have me leave a few years later? Here's the response I gave him: "I don't know if I'll ever get married. I do know how hard I've worked to get a good education and my MBA. I know how important it is to me to have a good career, and I know that will always be important to me." Although I didn't end up working for his organization, I did get asked back for a second interview. This happened a long time ago, but the lesson is still relevant today.

If you consider the 99,974 discrimination charges filed in 2011[1] in the United States, you can begin to understand why more organizations have moved toward more structured interviews. The number of discrimination charges in 2011 is more than 25 percent higher than it was in 2004, when I wrote the first edition of this book, so it is even more likely today for organizations to use structured interviews. Giving interviewers a list of questions to choose from that have already been vetted by a human resources or legal department can significantly reduce the chance that rogue interviewers will ask illegal questions that lead to discrimination charges or lawsuits. One significant benefit of competency-based interviews in particular is that they reduce the probability that an interviewer will ask an illegal or inappropriate question.

Of course, most employers would say that their main advantage is their focus on the competencies the organization or department needs to be successful. Joe Gorczyca, a former senior director of human resources at HP, was responsible for human resources for the company's worldwide sales and global supply chain organizations. At HP, he said, "In addition to considering the competencies improving individual performance, we tried to focus on competencies that reinforced the corporate culture." If you think about all the potential benefits to an organization, it is easy to understand why structured, competency-based interviews have become the standard.

How Are Interviewers Trained Differently for Competency-Based Interviews?

In addition to covering interviewing basics and EEO and affirmative action concerns, training in competency-based interviewing focuses on the key competencies for a particular position and core competencies for the organization. Such training also helps the interviewer know exactly what to listen and look for, in order to assess the candidate more accurately.

One of the most important core competencies at Johnson & Johnson is **Integrity and Credo-Based Actions**. According to Uneeda Brewer-Frazier, the former director of management education and development at the company, "Because of the strong credo-based culture at Johnson & Johnson, we work hard to select people who treat other employees and customers with respect, don't cut corners and demonstrate integrity through their work and actions. It is so important within Johnson & Johnson that it really impacts every aspect of how we do business and how we treat people." Johnson & Johnson trains interviewers about competencies and provides them with an interview guide that includes a list of planned behavioral questions for each competency. Interviewers are encouraged to ask follow-up questions to probe for additional information when an explanation isn't complete or when the response is unusual or unclear.

After going through the introductions and clarifying some things in the candidate's background, the interviewer begins the main part of the interview with a competency-based question. In addition to the example included in this chapter, you might want to review the example in Chapter 1 on the competency **Results and Performance Driven**.

Integrity and Credo-Based Actions	
Lives and champions our credo-values; displays command of one's self and responsibilities; strong personal integrity; creates and maintains an environment of trust.	Key Examples ☐ Transparent—Doesn't hold back on what needs to be said. Shares information in a truthful manner. ☐ Trustworthy—Gains the trust of others through appropriate ethical behaviors. Behaves consistently in similar situations. ☐ Builds trust—Treats others with dignity and respect. Models the credo-values and holds others responsible for their actions.

Planned Behavioral Questions

1. Tell me about a time at work when you objectively considered others' ideas, even when they conflicted with your own.
2. We do not always work with people who are ethical or honest. Provide an example of a time when you saw another employee or direct report do something that you thought was inappropriate. What did you do? What happened?
3. Often there are people in an organization who deserve more credit than they receive. Tell me about a time when you were involved in a situation like this. How did you handle the situation?
4. Often it is easy to blur the distinction between confidential information and public knowledge. Can you give me an example of when you were faced with this dilemma? What did you do?
5. Describe a time when you were asked to do something at work that you did not think was appropriate. How did you respond?

Situation/Task	Action	Result

Communication: ______________________________

____

Results and Performance Driven Rating: ☐

Adapted from material provided by Johnson & Johnson, used with permission.

The interviewer is asked on the Johnson & Johnson form to write about the candidate's answers. Specifically, the interviewer is asked to look at the three main parts of any answer to a behavioral question: Situation/Task, Action, and Result (STAR). Because these three parts are looked at carefully by most interviewers from organizations using behavioral interviewing, it is important to understand what the interviewers need to identify.

1. **Situation/Task:** What is the basic situation, task, or problem that you are giving to answer the behavioral question? Expect to give the details. (Note: Some organizations use the word "Problem" instead of "Situation" or "Task.")
2. **Action:** What action did you take to make the situation better? What decisions did you make to handle the task or resolve the problem?
3. **Result:** What was the result of the action? How did it benefit the organization or your department? What did you learn that will help you perform even better in the future? Any major "lessons learned" for you or your organization? Did you make money for the organization? Did you save time?

Chapter 4 will go into more detail on responding effectively to behavioral questions using these three areas. (Johnson & Johnson calls it STAR. Many career counselors know this approach under the acronym PAR, or Problem—Action—Result. Others refer to it as Situation—Action—Result, but I'm not aware of any calling it SAR. When an organization wants to look at the result first, be aware that STAR can easily become RATS.) The more you can find out about the target position and what it takes to be successful in it before the interview, the more likely it is that you'll be able to give the interviewer strong answers that will help prove your competence.

In a competency-based interview at Johnson & Johnson, the interviewer is asked to look at the candidate's answers in each competency area and rank each one according to the following scale:

---

5 Much more than acceptable (significantly exceeds criteria for successful job performance)

4 More than acceptable (exceeds criteria for successful job performance)

3 Acceptable (meets criteria for successful job performance)

2 Less than acceptable (generally does not meet criteria for successful job performance)

1 Much less than acceptable (significantly below criteria for successful job performance)

Interviewers at J&J are also asked to assess candidates' communication skills, as shown here:

Communication—Clearly conveying information and ideas through a variety of media to individuals or groups in a manner that engages the audience and helps them understand and retain the message.

Key Actions

+	0	–	
❑	❑	❑	Organizes the communication
❑	❑	❑	Maintains audience attention
❑	❑	❑	Adjusts to the audience
❑	❑	❑	Ensures understanding
❑	❑	❑	Adheres to accepted conventions
❑	❑	❑	Comprehends communication from others

Communication Rating: ☐

Key Points for Chapter 3

If you know what the interviewer is looking for, you will have an advantage over your competitors.

Key Questions	Answers
Why is it important to know what the interviewer is looking for before you are interviewed?	It can give you a significant edge over other candidates. Try to identify the employer's needs first, then start thinking about how you can prove to the employer that you have experience and skills in these critical competency areas.
What do interviewers always look for?	The best candidate for the job.
What three main points cover what interviewers look for?	◆ Can you do the job? ◆ Will you do the job? ◆ How well you fit with their people, department, organization, and culture.

Key Questions	Answers
What are the protected classes under United States employment laws?	◆ Race. ◆ Sex. ◆ Age. ◆ Religion. ◆ Disability. ◆ Veteran status. ◆ Color. ◆ Ethnicity/national origin.
What is the best way to handle an illegal question?	◆ Put the question in context. ◆ Don't take it personally and don't get angry. ◆ Identify the business need underlying the question, and respond to that need in your answer.
Why have more organizations moved to structured, competency-based interviews?	Because they: 1. Reduce the chance that an interviewer will ask illegal questions during the interview. 2. Help interviewers focus on selecting candidates based on the competencies the organization needs to be successful. 3. Help organizations reinforce and strengthen their corporate culture.
What is included in competency-based interview training?	◆ Interviewing basics. ◆ EEO, affirmative action, legal and illegal questions. ◆ Key competencies for the position. ◆ Verbal and nonverbal communication. ◆ Assessing candidates on their competencies (including communication skills).
What are the three main parts of an answer to a behavioral question that a good interviewer will listen for?	1. Situation/Task/Problem 2. Action. 3. Result.
What are the acronyms used by interviewers to describe these three parts?	◆ PAR—Problem, Action, Result. ◆ STAR—Situation/Task, Action, Result.

S. Laib
TELL ME ABOUT A TIME WHEN YOU WERE ABLE TO DEFINE THE WORD "IS"...
RESUME
BILL CLINTON

Chapter 4

Expect Competency-Based Behavioral Questions

Plans are only good intentions unless they immediately degenerate into hard work.

—Peter Drucker

To take a small amount of license with Peter Drucker's quote, as a candidate you need to plan on working hard if you want to do well in a competency-based interview. Learning to field questions in this kind of interview isn't easy. Even if you know you are a good communicator, you can be ever better if you anticipate what will happen in the interview and, above all, *practice*. Active preparation is key. Actors rehearse their lines and movements for weeks, sometimes even months, before opening night or before filming begins for a movie. Medical students and doctors practice surgery techniques on cadavers. Before a particularly difficult surgery using a new technique, surgeons spend hours strategizing and planning. The best litigators work with mock juries and even go through mock trials before a major trial to help them anticipate the real jury's concerns and issues. The best coaches and players spend hours training, both physically and mentally; they identify the other team's strengths and weaknesses, review footage of their games, and then adjust their own game to improve their chances of winning.

Just as the best actors, doctors, lawyers, coaches, and players do, the best interviewees plan for their interviews and prepare. If they want to work at the most sophisticated companies and organizations, they know they need to anticipate competency-based behavioral questions. Even if they already work for a competency-based organization, they prepare for their interview thinking about the competencies needed for the new position, whether it is a promotion or a transfer. The best interviewees today expect behavioral interview questions targeting the competencies needed to be successful in the position. They focus on the most important competencies the employer is looking for, and then start thinking about how they can prove they are strong in each of these key competency areas.

What Are Competency-Based Behavioral Questions?

Competency-based behavioral questions are questions asking for examples from your past behavior and experience to help the interviewer assess how strong you are in key competency areas. Remember that the theory behind behavioral questions is that past behavior is the best predictor of future behavior. If the interviewer wants to predict whether you are going to be successful at something in the future, he or she needs to find out how successful you've been in the past. Essentially, competencies provide the interviewer with a target for behavioral interview questions. As an interviewee you need to be focused on that same target: competencies. If you work this process the right way, the competencies you've focused on are the same competencies the interviewer is targeting.

How Can You Best Respond to Behavioral Questions?

Remember that there are three parts to any good answer to a behavioral question:

1. Situation, task, or problem.
2. Action.
3. Result.

Good interviewers are trained to listen for these three components in any answer. At Johnson & Johnson, for example, interviewers are asked to take notes and provide the candidate's answers by these three areas on their interview evaluation form. (See pages 23 and 46 for examples of the company's evaluation forms for two leadership competencies.)

The best way to order these three parts depends on which part of the answer is the most important to the interviewer. If you are interviewing with someone who is very results-oriented, for example, then start with the result. If the most critical thing to the interviewer is an understanding of the process, start with the situation or the action. You'll need to spend some time thinking about what result or results will make your point most effectively to the interviewer and decision-makers. As with any good sale, you need to think about the customer's (read: the company's) wishes and needs first, and then make sure that you talk about what is most important to the interviewer, first.

What Is the Best Way to Prepare for Competency-Based Interview Questions?

Take the time to be strategic. Work through this list:

1. Look at the key competencies you've identified for the position you plan to interview for.
2. Think about your strongest accomplishments that prove your competence in each key competency area. Make sure to include at least a few accomplishments that aren't already on your resume.
3. Pick examples that show the highest level of competence possible—unless, of course, you are interested in interviewing for a position for which you are overqualified.
4. Think about how you can explain the accomplishment to the interviewer in a conversational manner.
5. Be reasonably concise but also complete in your answers.
6. Remember to be positive, and make sure your nonverbal communication supports what you are saying. Don't give the interviewer mixed messages. (For more on nonverbal communication, see Chapter 6.)

How Does This Work?

Here are a few examples to show you how to begin proving your own competence. I've chosen examples from different professional levels, from entry-level all the way up to C-level executive. In most cases, the examples the candidates chose to talk about also show they are strong in more than one competency area. See if any of them describe something you've done. Pay attention to the way the candidate gives the answer by picking the key points that are the most important to telling the story. Notice that:

- ★ These examples use conversational language.
- ★ The candidates stay focused, without going off on a tangent.

Let's look first at the competency, **Initiative**. Other competencies, with specific examples, are included in Chapter 5.

Initiative

Chief Financial Officer, healthcare company, interview with large hospital system

Question: Give me an example of a time when you were able to take the lead in changing financial policy or practice for your organization.

Situation/Problem:
When I became the Chief Investment Officer, the senior managers and board were used to taking very little risk with the investment portfolio. The problem at the time was that by playing it that conservatively, the returns were lower than I thought they should be.

Action:
I spent six months educating key senior managers and board members about the potential benefit of taking at least 15 percent of the portfolio and using hedge funds and other nontraditional investment strategies. I met with them one-on-one and presented my recommendations at the end-of-the-year board meeting.

Result:
With support from the Chief Financial Officer and the CEO, I persuaded the board to change the company's investment policy to allow up to 25 percent of the investment portfolio to be invested in hedge funds and more esoteric investments.

★

What competencies are demonstrated in this answer? In addition to showing initiative, the candidate clearly showed he performed at a high level in these major competencies:

- Achieves Results.
- Organizational Awareness/Political Savvy.
- Impact and Influence.
- Analytical Skills.
- Interpersonal Skills.
- Conceptual Skills/Strategic Agility.

Administrative Assistant, interview for executive secretary position

Question: Have you seen an opportunity to do something in your position that would really help your department run more effectively? Tell me about it.

Situation/Problem:
When I started working in the sales department, most of the sales representatives kept their own records, and each of the eight territory managers tracked the information in his/her own spreadsheet. The managers provided the information to me every week, and I was responsible for consolidating the data on a single spreadsheet. I could see that my

manager would have more complete and more current information if we standardized the spreadsheet department-wide and linked it directly to information the sales representatives entered into the system.

Action:

I talked to my manager about why our department should update the way we collected sales information. I suggested how to set this up and volunteered to help him update the system.

Result:

I worked with two of the territory managers to design a system that would work using Excel and Access, and had the new system in place in one month. They now have real-time information on the status of any sales prospect, which helps the managers make better decisions.

★

Other competencies shown in the candidate's answer include:

- Achievement/Results Orientation.
- Influencing Skills.
- Information Seeking.
- Interpersonal Skills.
- Analytical Skills.
- Organizing.

College Senior, computer engineering, interviewing for first job after graduation

As a college senior majoring in computer engineering, Brian had focused on keeping his 3.67 GPA at the University of Maryland and had had very little real work experience by the time I first met him. He finally realized that he should have tried to obtain more work experience while he was in school, and that his lack of work experience put him in a less competitive position in the job market. One of the best things about competency-based resumes and interviews is that candidates can choose examples of their competence from work, school, or volunteer activities. All applicable experience applies.

Question: Tell us about a time you demonstrated initiative in school.

Action/Result:

I worked as a key member of the team that won the best senior project in the computer engineering honors program this last year. That next week, the department head, who was teaching the class, asked me to review his article based upon our project, before he submitted it to the best technical journal in the field.

Situation/Problem:
In my senior honors class, our professor asked us to work in teams of four to decide on a project using the computer engineering skills we had learned in the program. Our group decided to build a robotic fertilizer spreader, and I took the initiative to take the lead with the computer engineering work on the hydraulic system design.

★

Other competencies demonstrated by the candidate in the answer include:

- Achieves Results.
- Analytical Skills.
- Information Gathering.
- Interpersonal Skills.

Communication Tips for Stronger Answers

After reviewing the different ways these candidates showed their initiative, are you beginning to think of the times you've proven that you can demonstrate initiative? It's all about preparing, practicing, and building the competency you need to be successful in your next interview. Before we go to the next chapter, here are a few more tips to make your answers even better:

1. Make sure you respond to the question being asked. Don't assume you understand the question before the interviewer is finished talking. Listen.
2. Be smart with the language you choose. When possible, make sure to include terminology used by your professional colleagues. Do some research on specific words or jargon used by the employer, and remember to include these words in your answers. Consider using competency-related language in your answer. Know synonyms for each key competency.
3. Expect follow-up questions to your answers for additional information. Do your homework and review the details of any project or assignment you plan on using as an example to provide evidence that you are competent in a key area. Be able to cite financials, statistics, and/or headcount information if they are relevant.

4. Once you have brought up a subject, any follow-up question related to your subject is fair. So be careful and choose examples you are willing to talk about in detail.
5. Use positive language when answering any question. This bears repeating because it's very important. Interviewers do not want to offer a job to someone who seems negative or who doesn't take responsibility for their actions. Don't be perceived as a victim: Even if something has happened *to* you, demonstrate what you learned from the experience.
6. Prioritize the parts of your answer and focus on what is most important to the interviewer first. This is simply the best way to ensure that an interviewer pays attention to and remembers the most convincing part of your answer. In Chapter 5, you'll be given some examples that will show you how to prioritize as effectively as possible.

Now you're ready to look at a few more examples of competency-based behavioral questions and learn more tips that will help you answer these questions more effectively. In the next chapter, you'll learn how to pick good examples to prove your competence in critical competency areas. It takes more than initiative to be successful! But keep using your initiative to learn the rest of what you're going to need to ace the next interview. In other words, just keep reading.

Key Points for Chapter 4

Competencies provide the interviewer with a target for behavioral interview questions. As an interviewee you need to focus on that same target: competencies.

Key Questions	Answers
Who prepares for interviews?	The best interviewees. Candidates who will probably get the offer.
What are competency-based behavioral questions?	Questions asking for examples of your past behavior and experience to help interviewers assess how strong you are in key competency areas.
What are the three components of any good answer to a competency-based interview question?	• Situation/Problem/Task. • Action. • Result.

Key Questions	Answers
What is the order in which you should discuss these three components?	It depends which part of the answer is the most important to the interviewer. What is most important to him/her should take priority over what is most important to you.
What is the best way to prepare for a competency-based interview question?	1. Identify the critical competencies for the position. 2. Think about your strongest accomplishments in each key competency area. 3. Consider how to explain the accomplishment to the interviewer using a conversational, informal tone. Be concise and complete in your answer. Don't forget to cover the three components. 4. Be positive, and make sure your nonverbal communication supports what you're actually saying.
What else should you consider when you're answering a competency-based interview question?	◆ Listen closely and respond to the question being asked. ◆ Be smart in the language you use. Remember to use professional language or jargon, and include terms showing that you are comfortable with and conversant in the terminology used in the organization. Use competency-related language. ◆ Be prepared to answer follow-up questions probing your initial answer for additional details or competency-related information. ◆ Choose examples you are willing to talk about in detail. ◆ Use positive language. ◆ Prioritize the parts of an answer: always make your most critical points first.

Chapter 5

Prove Competencies With Examples

Now that you've read the previous chapter, you know to expect competency-based interview questions when you interview at the best places to work—the most sophisticated companies, government agencies, and nonprofit organizations. You've started to figure out how to give good answers to these tough, more focused kinds of questions. Now we need to build on that knowledge. Most of us need to learn the alphabet before we learn to read. We go to school to learn before we start working. Most of us date someone before we get married. When we want to start a new exercise regimen, most of us start slow and gradually build up our strength and endurance over time. (Of course there are always exceptions to these rules. I will always remember one of my favorite HR managers coming into the office and telling me that he'd just run three miles on his very first run. He told me he couldn't understand why he was so sore, or why I said, "You did *what?*" and started laughing.)

In this chapter, you'll learn how to avoid potential problems when you craft answers to questions targeting certain competencies. It's always good to know what to look for when you plan on flying over the Bermuda Triangle! You'll also learn some more ideas about how you can be even more savvy about choosing your best answers to competency-based behavioral questions. How can you identify stronger examples? How can you learn to prioritize what you say so that the interviewer listens to and understands the most important point?

Let's Get Ready

First, review the critical competencies. Make sure you understand what it takes to be successful in your professional area and the position you are interested in. Next, identify your best examples to provide evidence that you are strong in each key competency. If you are having trouble coming up with good examples, just ask for help. Your mentors, colleagues, managers, family, and friends may remember some things you've done that demonstrate how competent you are. Only ask people you know will have good things to say about you. Note: Some people seem to have a difficult time talking about their strengths; they see it as bragging. Modesty is never a virtue in an interview. To be effective in an interview, you need to get over the feeling that it is not okay to talk about your accomplishments. It's not only okay—it's essential.

Modesty is never a virtue in an interview.

Let's start by looking at some examples that real candidates have used to answer competency-based interview questions targeting the competencies **Ethics and Integrity** and **Customer Service**—two of the most commonly used and most valued competencies today, according to the Hay Group's Signe Spencer. Thoughtful and complete answers to specific competency-based questions targeting these two competencies can make a definite difference in how the interviewers will perceive you.

Ethics and Integrity

Let's say you are interested in interviewing for a position at a company or organization that you know values credibility, ethics, and integrity. Naturally, you would first need to think of examples that prove you're highly ethical and honest and have integrity. What you choose to talk about matters—especially when you're talking about integrity and honesty. However, people seem to have different definitions of these words. Even philosophers have struggled with answering the question, "What is honesty?" To illustrate this point, I've chosen someone I know very well who considers herself quite honest. How many times has she told others how good they look when she sees them—when she really doesn't think they look good? In her opinion, these white lies aren't dishonest, as long as she's achieved the purpose of making the other person feel better.

In almost every case you'll need to strike the right balance between showing that you are honest and trustworthy without seeming judgmental or self-righteous. Most interviewers will respond well to candidates who can matter-of-factly explain what they have learned that will help them make better decisions in the future. Self-righteousness is usually perceived as a definite negative, although this may depend on the personality of the interviewer, the position, and the overall culture of the organization. Again, do your homework!

Human Resources Professional, interview for HR position, Fortune 500 chemical company

> **Question:** Describe a time when you were asked to do something at work that you did not think was appropriate. How did you respond?

Situation:
I was working on finalizing a chart showing the employee headcount for the 15 facilities within the division. It was more difficult than usual because the organization was in the process of going through a restructuring, and transfer and termination dates changed daily. When I explained the situation, my manager told me to "make up the numbers if you have to."

Action:
I asked if he could wait 45 minutes—I thought I'd be able to confirm the real numbers by then. He agreed to wait.

Result:
I gave him a chart showing accurate employee headcount information 30 minutes later. (Note: Use an example that shows that you exceeded your deadline, if possible.)

★

College senior, nursing: interview for labor and delivery nurse at a large teaching hospital

> **Question:** Describe a time when you were in a situation in which you felt something you were asked to do was wrong, unethical, or inappropriate. How did you respond?

Situation:
When I worked as a student nurse at the University Medical Center, I told one of the nurses on the graveyard shift that we needed to get a doctor to sign the order to continue restraints for an alcohol withdrawal patient. She told me that the order wasn't necessary.

Action:
I called my professor to ask for advice because I wasn't comfortable ignoring the hospital's policy. Then I decided to go ahead and call the doctor to get the signature before the other order expired.

Result:
I was able to make sure we followed the hospital policy—it just made sense to me.

★

Experienced attorney: interview for appointment in U.S. Army Judge Advocate General's Corps

Question: Tell me about a time when you had to do something you didn't necessarily agree with.

Situation:
I worked defending a doctor practicing internal medicine who had been accused of medical malpractice by a patient for her failure to diagnose lupus in the early stages of the disease. The patient was very sympathetic, but I knew it was my job to represent the doctor.

Action:
Despite feeling some sympathy for the plaintiff, I stayed focused on the case and represented my client, the doctor, as well as I could.

Result:
The case settled out of court. My client told me she was very happy with my work and thought I had done a good job of representing her.

Customer Service

When you think about this competency, many of us think first about customer service professionals. We don't always realize that almost all of us have customers and clients, whether they are the internal customers within our organization or the external customers who keep our organization in business. Customers buy our products, use our services, and basically make our whole organization successful. Our internal customers and clients, including the people we report to and the departments we support, can also have a direct effect on our careers. Clearly this is an important competency for most positions.

Auditor: interview at a Fortune 500 company

Question: Describe a time when you worked on an audit and had to deal with some resistance from the people in the department or company you were auditing.

Situation:
I was assigned to work on a financial audit of 12 retail sites in Los Angeles for one of the major home improvement retail chains. At one of the

locations, when I asked for certain inventory records, the employees told me that they were not available. Other information was also "not available."

Action:

I spoke first with the store manager and told him about the lack of support I was receiving from the employees. He suggested that I talk with the employees at the store meeting at the beginning of the next shift. I explained to the employees that my job was to conduct the audit, and I'd appreciate their help. I asked if they had any questions about how the audit process worked, and answered a few of their questions.

Result:

I was able to complete the audit and developed a good relationship with managers and supervisors at that particular store.

★

Director of fundraising: interview for vice president of fundraising at a national organization's headquarters

> **Question:** Tell me about a time you persuaded a donor to contribute to the organization even though the first answer was no.

Result:

We just found out two weeks ago that one of the largest foundations in the city is donating $500,000 to the nonprofit's capital campaign.

Situation:

As a fundraiser, I've learned to never take no as an answer until I've heard it at least three times. So I'm used to having the first response be negative. Last year, we were told no for the second time by the foundation.

Action:

I talked to one of the women I know who is heading a major fundraising campaign for the nonprofit and asked for her advice. She's very powerful, runs a major law firm, and knows most of the important people in the city. She told me to call one of the key players on the foundation board and use her name. I went to lunch with the board member three times during the next six months, asked for advice, and made the case for donating to the nonprofit.

★

Waitress/high school graduate: interview for floor manager position at a chain restaurant

> **Question:** Tell me about a time when you used your best customer service skills.

Situation:
We were opening the restaurant for lunch one day last December, and the back section of the restaurant was really cold. One of the customers asked to speak to the floor manager to ask why they were seating people in such a cold room. I told the floor manager about the problem, and he went to speak to the customer. I looked at the customer while she was talking with the floor manager, and I could tell she wasn't happy.

Action:
After the floor manager left, I talked with the customer and asked if there was anything I could do. I offered her a hot drink and soup, and I didn't charge her for them.

Result:
The customer talked to our regional vice president in Dallas and explained what had happened. Our restaurant manager showed me the letter she wrote talking about what a good job I had done handling a difficult situation.

Focus on Organizations That Match Your Values

Imagine how helpful it would be to know something about the employer's values first, before you address your own ethics in an interview. The interviewers will be assessing whether your definitions of integrity and ethics fit their culture, so make sure you do your homework and find out how well the organization's values match your own. Start paying attention to public information about the organization and what people are saying about it. Every year, big corporations are ranked based on corporate reputation. In Houston, where I live, people who were listening to their personal network contacts heard questions and rumors about Enron's reputation several years before the scandal broke and became international news. Make sure you choose to listen, too.

Giving Good Answers to Competency-Based Interview Questions

Now that you've read through the answers that quality candidates gave to competency-based questions targeting **Customer Service**, **Ethics and Integrity**, and **Initiative**, are you starting to get a little more comfortable with the process? What did these answers have in common? As it turns out, quite a bit:

- ★ They're good at explaining the situation, action, and result in enough detail that the interviewer can follow the story, but not so much detail that the interviewer loses the main points.

- ⋆ They're focused on the most important points the interviewee thinks are the most critical to the interviewer. In some cases, you'll have to make an educated guess about which points are going to matter the most to the interviewer.
- ⋆ The three parts of each answer are prioritized based on the industry or professional area and the interviewer's style and choice of questions. Sales and fundraising, for example, are highly results-driven professional areas. Some interviewers are so direct and to the point that if you want a chance at getting the job, you'll need to give them the bottom-line result first.
- ⋆ In all of the answers, the interviewee has emphasized the most important or relevant point first. Don't wait until the end of your answer to give the interviewer your best point—the interviewer may have stopped listening by then!
- ⋆ Their tone is conversational, not formal or stilted. Many people automatically become more formal in an interview, both in the words they choose and the way they couch things. This can be a huge mistake because it can make you seem unapproachable or even haughty. Remember that they will be trying to assess how well you will fit into their organization or department.
- ⋆ The accomplishments that the interviewees discuss are uncontroversial, and help the interviewers perceive them as smart and savvy. They prove the interviewee's competence in the key areas needed to be successful in the organization.

Avoiding Potential Problems

So how can you increase your chance of success in a competency-based interview? Whenever possible, choose examples that will increase the chance you will be perceived in a positive way by the interviewer, and avoid giving examples that could make the interviewer perceive you in a negative way or as a victim. Whenever possible, take ownership of things that have happened at work that are your responsibility. Be professional, and don't blame others—even if they *deserve* the blame. When you are asked point-blank about failures or mistakes you have made, always tell the interviewer what you have learned from the experience that will make you more successful in the future.

Think about each of your accomplishments from different competency perspectives. This is important because it will help you be ready to answer questions about different competencies. Almost every accomplishment can be explained differently, simply by emphasizing different parts of the accomplishment. Identify the competencies that are at play in your examples, and consider how you would change your answer depending on which competency you are asked about. Remember to talk about what matters to the interviewer first and make your most important points first.

Be fairly direct in your answers. Being evasive or vague might work for politicians, but it will rarely help you in an interview. If necessary, take the time to gather your thoughts if you're not sure how to respond. Ideally, this should only happen once or twice if you've really done your homework and prepared. Many interviewees get themselves into trouble because they just jump in and start talking—even when they haven't thought through their answer. (This is something you are more likely to do if you are an extrovert like me.) If you prepare for a competency-based interview correctly, you should be able to answer almost all of the questions the interviewer asks. Taking the interview seriously—taking the time to prepare—will make all the difference.

Finally, *practice.* Find someone who is a savvy career coach, manager, or human resources professional who can help you fine-tune your answers to competency-based interview questions. Please check them out thoroughly and make sure they are really competent. Many coaches and consultants think they are more sophisticated and knowledgeable than they really are.

Recap

When you're getting ready for your next competency-based interview, make sure you start with a list of the competencies for the position. Then go through the list and identify the accomplishments you are most proud of and which provide evidence that you are strong in each competency area. Think about what you want to emphasize and how to explain the answer in a clear and organized, yet conversational way. Recognize that there are different ways to give the answer, depending on which competency you want to emphasize. Make sure you have included the three main parts of any good answer—situation/task, action, and result—and consider the order in which you will talk about them. Whatever will make your point most effectively is what you should talk about first. My best advice? Don't wait for your next interview. Start working on your list of competency-based accomplishments now.

Key Points for Chapter 5

Modesty is never a virtue in an interview.
Being evasive or vague might work for politicians, but it will rarely help you in an interview.

Key Questions	Answers
How can you prove your competencies?	Give the best examples from your experience that demonstrate the competencies that are important for the job.
What's the best way to prepare for a competency-based interview?	◆ Review the critical competencies. Make sure you understand what it takes to be successful in your own professional area and in the position you are interested in. ◆ Identify your best examples to provide evidence that you are strong in each key competency. ◆ If it is difficult to develop good examples, ask your mentors, colleagues, managers, family, and friends to describe instances in which they have seen you demonstrate particular competencies.
How can you find organizations whose values and core competencies match your own?	Look for news stories and surveys on corporate reputation. Talk to your network of colleagues and friends to learn more about an organization you are interested in. Listen.
What are the key characteristics of good answers to competency-based interview questions?	Good answers: ◆ Explain the situation, action, and result in enough detail that the interviewer can tell what the interviewee is talking about, but not so much detail the interviewer loses the main point. ◆ Focus on the points that are most critical to the interviewer. ◆ Emphasize the most important or relevant point by talking about it first. ◆ Couch everything in a conversational, informal tone. ◆ Show you are a smart, savvy employee—steer away from controversy. Always focus on the key competencies needed for success in the organization.

Key Questions	Answers
How can you avoid potential problems in the interview?	◆ Choose examples that help you present yourself in the most positive light. ◆ Avoid examples that could cause the interviewer to perceive you in a negative way or as a victim. Take ownership of everything that was your responsibility. Don't blame others, even if they deserve the blame. ◆ Respond to questions about failures or mistakes by talking about what you have learned and how that will make you more successful in the future. ◆ Think about each accomplishment from the perspective of different competencies. Almost every accomplishment can illustrate more than one competency, depending on which part is emphasized. ◆ Remember to talk about what matters to the interviewer first. ◆ Be direct, and answer the interviewer's questions. ◆ If you need to gather your thoughts, take a moment to do so. This shouldn't happen more than twice in any interview if you have really done your homework and are prepared. If you are well-prepared you should be able to answer most of the questions. ◆ Find a professional to help you fine-tune your answers. Make sure the person you choose understands competency-based interviewing.

Chapter 6

Present Yourself as a Strong Candidate

Even the smallest person can change the course of history.

—Galadriel in *The Lord of the Rings: The Fellowship of the Ring*

You've worked hard and thought about good answers to behavioral questions targeting the competencies for the particular position you are interested in. That's the first step to being successful in a competency-based interview. But it is only the first step. You also need to look the part, act the part, and present yourself as a strong candidate. In this chapter, I'm going to cover the basics of nonverbal communication, which you'll need in order to do well in any interview. Then I'm going to look at how you can use nonverbal communication to your advantage in competency-based interviews. Nonverbal communication will always play a large part in your performance in any interview, including competency-based interviews. So just what is nonverbal communication? It's every type of communication we use to send a message except the actual words we choose.

Nonverbal Communication

Nonverbal communication is very important in any interview. In addition to having thoughtful, competency-based answers at your disposal, you will also need to:

- Maintain good eye contact.
- Dress appropriately.
- Use the right gestures.
- Have a firm handshake.
- Behave appropriately.

- ★ Smile at appropriate times.
- ★ Respect your interviewer's personal space.
- ★ Respond to your interviewer's nonverbal communication.
- ★ Avoid giving mixed messages, in which your nonverbal communication contradicts your words.
- ★ Deliver your answers in an organized way.
- ★ Converse with your interviewer in an informal manner.

Looking the part starts with dressing appropriately. Even though you may want to dress according to the culture of the organization or the location of the interview, you will almost always be perceived as dressing appropriately if you dress on the conservative end of the range for your professional area or industry. You want the interviewer to remember you because you're impressive, not because of what you wore.

Pay attention to your voice and diction. Make sure your interviewer can hear you but that you aren't screaming at her. Speak clearly, put some energy and life in your voice, and use good grammar. Try to minimize the number of pauses and what communication experts call *dysfluencies*—the *uhs, ums, you knows, so's*, and *likes* that sometimes interfere with conversation.

If you've ever taken a communication class in high school or college (or if you are simply a smart, observant person), you probably already know how important nonverbal communication is in any interaction. First impressions matter, and the interviewer's first impression is based on nonverbal communication. Most interviewers make up their minds quickly about candidates—within the first 15 seconds to two minutes of the interview. Clearly, nonverbal communication can make a significant difference in any interview.

One of my clients, someone with 10 years of experience and a PhD from one of the top U.S. engineering programs in his field, told me he'd never done well in interviews. When I met him, he sat on the edge of his chair, leaned forward, and slightly bounced as he talked. I videotaped him so he could see for himself what he was doing. I explained to him about how important it was to not invade the interviewer's space; I told him to sit back in his chair, with his back straight, and to stop bouncing. He followed the advice and received an offer after the next interview.

You've probably heard the saying that "actions speak louder than words." Every culture seems to have an equivalent saying, so know that nonverbal communication is important worldwide. Because nonverbal communication is influenced by the surrounding culture, what is considered appropriate in one country may be seen very differently in another. For example, direct eye contact is expected in the United States and is looked at as a sign of honesty and trustworthiness. In certain countries in Africa and Asia, however, direct eye contact is a sign of disrespect. If you live or work in one of the more diverse cities in the United States, as I do, or in another country, you may want to learn about these cross-cultural differences. If you use nonverbal communication appropriately in your interview and try to be sensitive to the cultural expectations of your interviewer, it can only work in your favor.

In this chapter, the examples and explanations are based on the cultural expectations and morés of the United States. If you live in another country or plan to interview with an organization based in another part of the world, please take the time to learn what is expected of a good interviewee there—in other words, what the interviewers would consider appropriate in terms of nonverbal communication. (Refer to Chapter 12 for more information on global issues, including nonverbal communication, with competency-based interviews.) Many places are farther away from Kansas than Oz was for Dorothy. But at least the Munchkins spoke and sang in English, and the Wizard was from Omaha.

Competency-Based Interviews and Nonverbal Communication

When you're getting ready for a competency-based interview, one of the most important things to remember is to consider the interviewer's and the employer's needs first. By first identifying the competencies the employer needs to be successful, you can begin to think about your own accomplishments to prove you are strong in each competency area.

Your nonverbal communication needs to be consistent with what you are saying, too. You can't expect an interviewer to respond positively to your well-crafted, competency-based answer if you are rolling your eyes upward as you speak. When your nonverbal message contradicts your verbal message, interviewers will believe the nonverbal message. This is true worldwide. So when you tell the interviewer you are willing to relocate but your head is shaking "no," the interviewer, with good reason, is going to question your words and believe the headshake. When you give an interviewer this type of mixed message, you may appear untruthful. Good interviewees don't give mixed messages in the interview.

What kind of nonverbal communication really matters during a competency-based interview? To provide you with especially helpful tips, I'm going to cover anything that could influence the interviewer's perception of you other than the specific accomplishments and the words you are using in your answers. Let's look at three of the most common competencies and think about the verbal and nonverbal communication we would expect, competency by competency. Please remember that expectations, styles, and traditions vary from culture to culture, so if you plan to interview in a country whose culture differs from your own, you should first speak with someone who truly understands how people communicate there. Knowing what interviewers expect in that sense will help you assess your own verbal and nonverbal communication strengths and weaknesses.

Note: If you know there are often discrepancies between your verbal and nonverbal responses, you may choose to either adjust your answers, change your attitude, or ask a friend, coach, or other professional to help you understand what might be behind the mixed message. The goal is to make your verbal and nonverbal messages more consistent with one another.

Achievement/Results Orientation

What can interviewees do or say to help prove to interviewers that they are results oriented? In many cases, the interviewer himself might not recognize the specific details that helped him come to his conclusion about a candidate's strength (or lack thereof) in this area. Think about the evidence an interviewer would look for in order to feel convinced that an interviewee is focused on performance, goals, objectives, or results. Some of this key evidence will be verbal—the words the candidate uses. And some of this evidence will be nonverbal. This includes how the candidate:

- ★ Talks.
- ★ Maintains eye contact.
- ★ Handles body language.
- ★ Dresses.
- ★ Grooms and takes care of himself.

Does the candidate explain the results using numbers, statistics, dollars, time spent, or some other measurement to help the interviewer understand the size or scope of the accomplishment? Someone strong in this competency would. An astute interviewer would expect the answers from a results-oriented candidate to be organized, logical, concise, and complete. The emphasis in some of their most important answers would be on the results instead of the process. The interviewer would be able to tell that it was a priority for the candidate because:

- The result would be given near the beginning of the answer.
- More time would be spent explaining the result than the situation/task/problem or action.

What else helps confirm the candidate is strong in the **Achievement/Results Orientation** competency? A good interviewer would expect a results-oriented person to get to the point quickly. She would generally not be guilty of wasting the interviewer's time by going off on tangents or focusing on details that aren't critical. She would maintain good eye contact. She would be engaged in the conversation. The interviewer would be able to assess all of this through her gestures, her facial expressions, and her posture. (A note on posture: If you lean too far forward in the chair it can look as though you're invading the interviewer's space—or you'll simply seem strange.) Think of people you know who achieve results—what other nonverbal cues would *you* expect to see in this type of candidate?

Impact and Influence

An interviewer would expect to see many of the same nonverbal cues we discussed for **Achievement/Results Orientation**. An interviewee demonstrating his influencing strengths would maintain good eye contact, would remain engaged in the conversation, and would sit and stand appropriately. There are some subtle differences, however. Remember that this is the competency that describes a candidate's ability to persuade, convince, impact, and influence the right people in order to be successful. Think about people who are called aggressive versus those who are assertive. Assertive people are equally people-focused and task-focused; aggressive people tend to focus on achieving the goal. Compare the competencies needed for selling based on strong, long-term relationships and those needed for selling based on immediate contact and volume. People with strong influencing skills are almost always assertive, not aggressive. They recognize they will need to work with the same people in the future, so they try to protect the relationship whenever possible.

What evidence will help convince an interviewer that a candidate has strong influencing skills? The most important thing is the way the candidate answers questions and targets the interviewer's real needs, or even asks the interviewer questions to clarify those needs. He should emphasize the fact that he has what the interviewer is looking for, that his experience will help ensure his success in the new position—in other words, that he knows how to sell himself and his ideas *without overselling*. People with strong influencing skills know how to read people and convince them to change their position, now or somewhere down the line. If they are really subtle and clever, they can even make the other person think that the change is his/her own idea. They can use a short tangent or tell a story, just to help them persuade someone to change his or her viewpoint.

Candidates with strong influencing skills also tend to have a good sense of humor. Knowing how to come up with a good one-liner or tell a joke at the right time can help relieve tension, persuade a colleague, or close a deal. (A word of warning: Always be appropriate. You need to make sure you are not the only one who finds something funny.)

Integrity and Ethics

What verbal and nonverbal cues will help an interviewer assess how strong (or weak) a candidate is in the competency **Integrity and Ethics**? Astute interviewers may feel that a candidate is lying when he/she:

- ★ Gives examples that don't make sense or contradict each other.
- ★ Exhibits nonverbal communication that contradicts his/her words.
- ★ Fidgets and avoids eye contact at certain relevant times.
- ★ Moves less frequently than truthful candidates.
- ★ Talks more slowly and makes more errors than most candidates.
- ★ Uses fewer words when answering questions, often one-word answers with little elaboration.
- ★ Uses longer pauses, both before and while answering.
- ★ Uses more "generalizing terms" such as *you know what I mean* and *you know* at the ends of sentences.
- ★ Uses fewer concrete terms and refers less frequently to specific people and places.
- ★ Guards or covers his or her mouth, touches his or her nose, and rubs his/her eyes.[1]

These are just some of the ways that good communicators can identify lying or deceit. Most good interviewer training encourages interviewers to look for *several* indicators that someone is lying; one indicator by itself is generally not enough to constitute proof. Even law enforcement officers need more than fidgeting and excessive pausing to build their case when they can tell that a suspect isn't telling the truth: They look for more evidence. That's what good interviewers do, too.

You'll generally do better as a candidate if you tell the truth during an interview—smart and savvy interviewers will probably be able to tell when you're lying anyway. Don't try to be someone you're not, because if you do get the offer, you may find yourself in a situation that isn't a good fit for the real you. As a coach, though, I'm a believer in diplomatic honesty, not brutal honesty. Tell the truth, but say it in a way that is more likely to help you than hurt you. Always put the best possible spin on everything you say. Here's an example: For the men reading this chapter, please know that you don't have to come out and tell the woman in your life that what she's wearing makes her look fat when she asks you. Just ask her what she thinks, or, better yet, tell her that she always looks good to you.

When you think about all the nonverbal cues that can cause you to be perceived as dishonest, you'll begin to realize why I have encouraged you to give specific, concrete answers to competency-based questions, and to prepare, so you can think about what to say before the actual interview. By taking the time to get ready for a competency-based interview, you'll increase the chance that you won't need to pause or give the interviewer reason to think that you may not be telling the truth.

Trust me—I *am* telling you the truth!

Other Competencies

Now that you've learned how to support your answers to competency-based interview questions with good nonverbal communication for the competencies **Achievement/Results Orientation**, **Impact and Influence**, and **Integrity and Ethics**, you need to think about how to support the other relevant competencies through consistent nonverbal and verbal communication. For example, consider the competency **Customer Service**. Wouldn't you expect to see a good customer service or sales professional know when to:

- ★ Smile and demonstrate support and caring for a customer?
- ★ Pace his or her answers more slowly and use a calmer tone of voice when dealing with a difficult customer?

Think about what evidence you need to provide that will support your answers to competency-based interview questions targeting the *other* key competencies on your list for the target position or company.

Other Nonverbal Tips

We may be too old to grow except in pounds, worth, and wisdom. Some things that affect how we look can't be changed. But other things can. If you are a woman who wants to interview for a high-powered job, consider getting your makeup and hair done professionally and buying a new suit and shoes. If you need to lose some weight, start your diet and exercise program soon enough to make a difference by the time you interview. Get recommendations for makeup artists, manicurists, hair stylists, personal shoppers, and good places to shop from people you know who look polished and professional. It just may be worth the investment.

If you are a man, consider making some of the same extra effort, too. Good grooming and a professional, conservative look is important for both men and women.

Key Points for Chapter 6

Actions speak louder than words.

Key Questions	**Answers**
What is nonverbal communication?	Every type of communication except the actual words someone uses.
What nonverbal communication is important in any interview?	◆ Maintaining good eye contact. ◆ Dressing appropriately and conservatively. ◆ Using the right gestures. ◆ Having a firm handshake. ◆ Behaving appropriately. ◆ Smiling at appropriate times. ◆ Respecting personal space. ◆ Responding to the interviewer's nonverbal communication. ◆ Avoiding giving mixed messages. ◆ Talking with the interviewer in an organized, logical, yet conversational way, paying attention to voice and diction.

How does culture affect nonverbal communication in an interview?	Expectations and styles vary according to the country/culture of the organization, and sometimes that of the interviewer, as well. Expect different nonverbal communication styles and conventions when interviewing across cultures, and be more sensitive to the expectations of your interviewer.
Key Questions	**Answers**
What would cause an interviewer to rate a candidate as strong in the competency **Achieve Results**?	◆ The candidate explains his/her results using quantitative and qualitative data. ◆ His/her answers are organized, logical, concise, and complete. ◆ More emphasis is placed on results than process; results seem to be a priority for the candidate. ◆ The candidate gets to the point quickly. ◆ He/she maintains good eye contact and remains engaged in the conversation.
What would cause an interviewer to believe that a candidate is strong in the competency **Impact and Influence**?	He or she will exhibit many of the same cues shown in the competency **Achieves Results**. In addition: ◆ He or she is assertive, not aggressive. Considers long-term relationships with others. ◆ Can sell his/her ideas effectively without overselling. ◆ Good at reading people. ◆ Good at understanding subtleties and using them to convince others. ◆ Uses stories and humor to help make points and persuade others to change their point of view.

What verbal and nonverbal cues will cause an interviewer to doubt a candidate's strength in the competency **Integrity and Ethics**?	• The candidate gives unclear or contradictory examples. • His/her words and nonverbal communication don't match up. • Fidgets and/or avoids eye contact, or, conversely, sits very still and moves less than other candidates. • Talks more slowly and make mistakes verbally. • Gives short answers with little elaboration. • Pauses often. • Uses general terms that imply limited knowledge. • Is general and vague. • Touches his/her nose, rubs his/her eyes, or covers his/her mouth.
Key Questions	**Answers**
How honest should you be in an interview?	Diplomatic honesty is best. There's no reason to be brutally honest. Put the best possible spin on things without actually being untruthful.
What else should you do to prepare for a competency-based interview?	• Go through your list of critical competencies for the position, and figure out how to present yourself as a strong candidate—verbally and nonverbally—in each competency area. • Make an effort to look as professional as possible the day of the interview. Consider losing weight or buying a new outfit. Pay attention to your grooming (have it done professionally, if possible), and make sure your shoes are shined. If you need further advice, ask someone you know who always looks polished and put-together.

Chapter 7

Consider Other Important Interview Tips

He who asks a question is a fool for five minutes; he who does not ask a question remains a fool forever.

—Chinese proverb

At this point, you've learned about how competency-based interviewing works, how to develop good answers to competency-based interview questions, and how to look and act like as the best candidate. You probably think you are ready for your next competency-based interview, and so do I—*almost*. Because we don't want to be fools forever, we'll follow the advice in the Chinese proverb and start by asking a question: What else do you need to know to get the offer? Despite the fact that competency-based interviewing is the most common approach to interviewing today, you may still have to field a few questions that are not strictly competency-based. Your job as the candidate is to do a good job of answering *all* of these questions.

Here are five examples of the other kinds questions you may be asked:

- ★ Why are you interested in this position?
- ★ Tell me about yourself.
- ★ What is your current salary? What salary do you expect?
- ★ What are your strengths?
- ★ What is your biggest weakness?

How should you answer these questions to do well in the interview? How can you use your knowledge of competency-based interviewing to give stronger answers to these other types of questions? After reading about how to answer these questions, you'll probably think you're ready to do well in your next interview. Please take the time to review the question-and-answer section at the end of this chapter. You may find that you get just one additional tip that will make all the difference in your next interview.

Answer Other Common Questions Showing Competency Strengths[1]

Why Are You Interested in This Position?

You are very likely to be asked this question (or a similar question with the same intent) before the interview is set up or during the interview itself. Even though this question doesn't seem like it would belong in a competency-based interview, interviewers may ask one or two questions that are not included in their approved competency-based interview guide. The best answers to this kind of question focus on how your experience and interests match the organization's needs. In other words, this is an opportunity to show you have the right competencies for the position and are interested in developing the competencies that are needed for the organization to be successful in the future.

Here's one possible response: "Three main reasons. It will give me the chance to prove how good I am at achieving goals; building strong, long-term relationships with customers; and motivating employees in the department to be even more successful." Paraphrase the competencies. Explain the relevant competencies in your own words using synonyms. Expect to give examples of how you've used these competencies in the past. Even when the question is not technically a behavioral question, using past behavior or examples will help provide proof to the interviewer that you will remain strong in these same competencies in the future. Again, always look for ways your experience and competencies fit or match the position. Research the position and the organization online. Ask people you know who work for the same organization or are in a similar position at a competitor.

Tell Me About Yourself

You have probably figured out by now that you should always emphasize the employer's needs first and your own, second. So what is a good answer to this question? Think about this: What is it about you that the employer needs to know to realize you have the competencies he/she needs to help the organization be more successful? Limit your answer to no more than two minutes, and make sure you focus on your work experience: Human resources managers tell unbelievable stories about candidates talking about their divorce, their problems with their children, or their health problems. Some interviewers have even told stories about candidates trying to convert them to another religion. You are a professional, and your answer to this question needs to stay professional. Avoid emphasizing your private, personal life. This is especially true in the United States.

But, as I've already mentioned, the way any interview is conducted, even a competency-based interview, is affected by the culture of the employer and the culture and laws of the country it is located in. In some other parts of the world you should expect questions about your personal life and then answer those questions—if you want to do well on the interview. One British company that hired me as a consultant was starting a subsidiary in the United States. The supervisors were surprised to learn that they shouldn't ask candidates about their marital status or family when they interviewed in the United States, because they routinely asked those questions in Europe.

The traditional answer to this question is chronological: Start from the beginning and work toward the present, emphasizing the aspects of your background that are the most relevant for the position. The second approach is to briefly discuss your early background and education, but spend most of the two minutes focused on your current strengths, skills, and abilities, and what you want to do next. Both approaches can work, but one may be more effective for you than the other, depending on your situation. Be logical, organized, and concise. Mention evidence of your competencies that are related to the position you are interviewing for when you are talking about your background—in this way, you'll send the message that you've been developing your competencies over time and that they are strong. Don't forget that the interviewer is probably evaluating your skills as a communicator while listening to the content of your answer.

What Is Your Current Salary? What Salary Do You Expect?

Many people are extremely uncomfortable answering questions about money during an interview. For many people, talking about money ranks right up there with religion, politics, and sex as topics they'd like to avoid. The way to address these questions is to focus on the employer's needs first. This is not just about you and what you think is appropriate for the interviewer to ask. Almost without exception, when interviewers ask these types of questions, they are doing it because they need to know. If they want to make you an offer, they need to come up with a salary that you will be happy with and that fits within the salary range of people in their organization with similar experience and skills. They are simply trying to be fair. If you *still* have a problem answering these kinds of questions, please work on getting over it. There is no way you can avoid discussing salary when you are interviewing for a job.

So what is a good way to answer these two questions? In most cases I coach my clients to answer the first question. As for the second, I encourage them to tell the interviewer, "I'm sure if you decide that I am the right person for the job that you will do the very best for me that you can." Guilt is a wonderful thing if it works in your favor.

Please be aware that this is only the first step in salary negotiation. To give really on-target advice, a consultant would need to know much more about the job opportunity and your own situation.

What Are Your Strengths?

When you answer this question, first focus on your strengths that match the competencies that are the most important to help the employer be successful in the future. Leave out any strengths that are not important for success in the position. For example, if you are very creative and have had your paintings shown in galleries, that type of competency might not be seen as an asset if you are interviewing for a position as an engineer.

Choose three or four of the most important competencies for the position that you are strong in, and answer the question using these competencies. Start with the competency that is most important to the interviewer's success, and then talk about your strength in the second most important area. Put the competencies in your own language because you will come across as more sophisticated than the next candidate, who may just repeat the competency list, word for word. Actually, you *will* be more sophisticated than the next candidate— after all, you're reading this book!

What Is Your Greatest Weakness?

Listen carefully to the question. Is the interviewer really asking for one weakness, or several? Most career consultants will tell candidates to answer this question by picking a weakness and turning it into a strength. That may be true most of the time, but to do this correctly, your answer should be diplomatically honest, original, and, above all, authentic. Stay away from the cookie-cutter answers such as "I'm a perfectionist," unless you can provide enough evidence to back up this claim. Remember that everyone has weaknesses; saying you do not have any weaknesses simply is not believable.

When you answer this question, it is important to choose a weakness that is unrelated to the critical competencies for the position. For example, you won't want to be perceived as being weak in **Analytical Skills**, if that is a key part of being successful in the position. Try to pick something that the interviewer may have already noticed as a weakness during the interview. One example: "I'm not always as concise as I think I should be. I'm aware that I need to be better about getting to the point faster, and I'm working on it. I know it is something I could improve." Think about how effective this answer would be for a candidate who has just gone off on a tangent during the interview. At least the interviewer is now aware that the candidate recognizes the problem.

Another approach is to focus on something different that might be a little humorous. One client from West Virginia was preparing for an interview in Texas, and he had a good sense of humor. His answer? "I don't know if you've noticed, but some people here think I have an accent. So they underestimate me. While they're doing this, they tell me all sorts of information before they figure out I really know what I'm doing. But occasionally this can work against me." Do you see why this answer worked well for him?

Competency Gaps

In addition to the weakness question, sometimes you may get a question about a competency that you know is not a strength for you—an area where you have a weakness, or *competency gap*. What can you do when you are unable to prove certain key competencies, or when you are not as strong as you need to be in a critical competency area? As a candidate, you should become more aware of your competency gaps and learn what to do to overcome those gaps. One way to handle this situation is to talk about how you have compensated for the competency gap by using your strength in another competency. For example, it might be difficult for you to come up with an example of how you've directly influenced or persuaded someone to change his or her position on an important issue—but you may be able to focus instead on an example of when you used strong customer service skills to satisfy a difficult customer. Another approach is to acknowledge the gap and then explain what you have done or plan to do to build your strength in that competency in the future. Have you signed up for a class or volunteered for a project at work that will give you the opportunity to prove that you are competent in the relevant area in the near future? If so, let the interviewer know.

Interview Questionnaire: True or False?

1. *The best-qualified candidate always gets the job.*
   False. Interviewers consider other things in addition to qualifications. They try to assess how willing you are to work hard and how well you'll fit

into their department and organization. In competency-based organizations, interviewers also assesses how strong you are in the competencies needed to be successful in the job. In addition, interviewers may be persuaded to make an offer to someone who can benefit them politically—say, the nephew of the CEO.

2. *It's a good idea to schedule your first interviews for the positions you are the most interested in.*
   False. Most interviewees don't do as well in their first interviews as they will in later interviews, when they are more comfortable with the process. So try to have a "practice" interview (or work with a coach or career consultant) before you have one that really matters to you.
3. *The first few minutes of the interview are the most important.*
   True. Most interviewers make up their minds quickly.
4. *You should wear conservative clothes to an interview.*
   True. But make sure what you wear is considered conservative for your professional area or industry—not someone else's. It is important to wear conservative clothes because you want the interviewer to remember you for your professionalism and intelligence and the quality of your answers—not for the clothes you wore. If the interviewer remembers you for your clothes, that is *not* a good thing.
5. *Take a planner and a notepad to the interview.*
   Trick question. Take them with you but don't take notes during the interview. If you do take notes, the interviewer may perceive you as having a poor memory, as inattentive (less eye contact), or perhaps even as interested in getting him/her into trouble (think of a potential discrimination charge or lawsuit). Take some notes on your notepad or in your planner immediately after the interview so that you can write more effective thank-you notes.
6. *It's always good to arrive 20 to 30 minutes early for the interview.*
   False. In most cases, you should plan to arrive about five minutes early. If you arrive earlier, you may actually inconvenience the interviewer, who will not be expecting you a half hour early. Although it is always better to be early rather than late, too early isn't good, either. Get to the location early but wait in your car, downstairs, or across the street in a restaurant until it's the right time to go to the interview. As you wait, review your resume and check to make sure you are still looking as professional as you did after you first dressed for the interview.
7. *When asked to talk about your background, you should plan to keep your response to about two minutes.*
   True. Don't be too brief—*or* too wordy. Watch the interviewer's nonverbal communication; if he or she looks bored, pick up the pace of your answer and finish talking. Emphasize the competencies that are critical for the position.

8. *During an interview, avoid making too much eye contact to help the interviewer feel less nervous.*
   False. Maintaining good eye contact is perceived positively in interviews in the United States. Just don't stare! Remember that the rules for eye contact may be different in other parts of the world, especially parts of Africa and Asia. So make sure you've done your research and know what's expected.
9. *It is best to be honest and tell the interviewer exactly how you felt about previous supervisors if you are asked for your opinion.*
   False. Remember that diplomatic honesty is better than brutal honesty. If you talk negatively about a former supervisor, the interviewer will think that you will be talking negatively about him or her in the future. So be professional and discreet.
10. *Don't answer questions about race, sex, age, national origin, marital status, or number of children.*
    Trick question. It depends. Put the question in context and respond considering the underlying reason for the question. See page 43 in Chapter 3 for more details.
11. *What you say counts for more than the interviewer's perception.*
    False. Perception is reality. The interviewer will make a decision based on her perception of how successful you will be in the job as compared to other candidates. So it is up to you to communicate what you mean as clearly as you can so that you increase the chance that the interviewer will perceive you accurately.
12. *Exaggerate your accomplishments, because the interviewer won't be able to tell that you're not telling the truth.*
    False. A perceptive interviewer will be able to tell when you are not telling the truth based on your nonverbal and verbal communication. Make your best case but make sure you stay honest.
13. *Your job in the interview is to sell yourself.*
    True. Your whole job in the interview is to persuade the interviewer that you deserve a second interview or a job offer.
14. *Preparing for an interview is a waste of time.*
    False. Preparing for an interview is the best use of your time—if you care about being seriously considered for the opportunity.

Key Points for Chapter 7

When you think you're ready, do a little more.

Key Questions	Answers
Will all the questions in a competency-based interview be competency-based behavioral questions?	Not necessarily. Even in a competency-based interview, you may need to field a few questions that are not traditional, competency-based interview questions.
What should you keep in mind when you answer the question "Why are you interested in this position?"	Focus on how your experience and interests match the competencies the employer is looking for. A strong candidate gives specific examples to support what he or she is saying. Use synonyms to describe competencies. Paraphrase and explain things in your own words.
When the interviewer asks you to tell him about yourself, what should you say?	◆ Key point: What about you does the employer need to know to realize you have the right competencies to help the organization be successful? ◆ Limit your answer to two minutes. Be logical, organized, and concise. ◆ Focus on your professional experience that is relevant to this position, not on your personal life. ◆ Follow the traditional chronological approach, or briefly discuss your background and education, focusing on your current strengths and competencies and what you want to do next.
How should you answer questions about salary?	◆ Be open about your current salary if you're asked, unless there's a good reason not to. Don't feel uncomfortable talking about money. ◆ If you're asked about salary expectations, say, "I'm sure if you decide I'm the right person for the job that you will do the very best you can for me."

Key Questions	Answers
What are the most important things to remember when asked to identify your strengths?	◆ Emphasize your strengths that match the competencies the employer needs to be successful in the future. ◆ Choose three or four of the relevant competencies for the position that you consider to be your strengths. ◆ Start your answer with the competency that has the greatest weight or is the most important to the employer. ◆ Paraphrase and use synonyms to describe the competencies to the employer. Put the relevant competencies in your own words. ◆ Be certain whether you are being asked about a strength or *strengths*, in which case you'll have to provide at least two examples.
How should you answer the question, "What is your biggest weakness?"	Most career consultants tell their clients to pick a weakness and turn it into a strength. To do this correctly, you should: ◆ Be diplomatically honest, not brutally honest. ◆ Be original and authentic. ◆ Choose a weakness that is unrelated to the key competencies for the position you are interviewing for. ◆ Remember that even the best employees have weaknesses: d*o not* answer this question by saying that you have no weaknesses. ◆ Select a weakness that the interviewer may have already noticed during the interview. ◆ Consider picking an example that shows humor and that you are human. Just make sure you're not the only person who thinks it's funny.
What is a competency gap?	A competency you can't prove or one that you don't have.

Key Questions	Answers
How can you answer questions about such gaps?	◆ Talk about how you have compensated for the competency gap by using your strength in another competency. ◆ Acknowledge the competency gap and explain to the interviewer what steps you have taken to overcome it (for example, signing up for a class or a volunteer project or asking to participate in a relevant project at work).
What are some other basic tips that you need to know in order to do well in the interview?	◆ Recognize that the best-qualified candidate doesn't always get the offer. ◆ Schedule interviews for the positions you are the most interested in after you have had some interviews and know that you are handling the interview well. ◆ The first few minutes of an interview are the most important. Do everything you can to create a good first impression. ◆ Wear clothes that are considered conservative for your professional area or industry. ◆ Don't take notes during the interview. Do this after the interview so you can write more effective thank-you notes. ◆ Plan to arrive for the interview five to 10 minutes early. ◆ Maintain polite eye contact during the interview. ◆ Be professional and discreet when talking about previous or current employers. ◆ Put any illegal or inappropriate questions in context; consider the interviewer's underlying reason for asking the question. ◆ The interviewer will make decisions based on his/her perception of you as a candidate. ◆ Tell the truth but be diplomatic. ◆ Your job is to sell yourself. ◆ Preparation is extremely important—if you want an offer.

Mid-Book Review

To make sure you are ready for the interview, here is a helpful checklist of all the major points discussed in the first seven chapters. In the boxes provided, write the applicable page number(s) and the date you complete each "lesson."

Step 1: Understand Competency-Based Interview Approaches

Key Questions and Tasks	Reference Page	Date Completed
Know how a competency-based interview is different from other interviews.		
Review the information about competency-based behavioral interviewing. Begin thinking about how your own behavior has contributed to your success in the past.		
Remember that behavioral interviewing is based on the theory that past behavior is the best predictor of future behavior.		

Step 2: Identify the Right Competency List

Key Questions and Tasks	Reference Page	Date Completed
Review the job advertisement looking for competencies. They may be listed directly as competencies or as success factors, dimensions, or values. Ask for a job description from a recruiter and see whether the organization has identified competencies as part of that description.		
If the competencies aren't clearly identified in the advertisement or job description, follow these four major steps to develop a list on your own: 1. Think about the obvious competencies for the position. 2. Look at competitors' advertisements and job postings. 3. Check for competencies from other sources, such as employment Websites, newspapers ads, magazines and journals, professional associations, and the organization's own Website. 4. Select 10 to 15 competencies that would be most critical from Appendix A. *As you research competencies for the position, remember that the competency-based interview approach always looks at the employer's needs first. Your task is to think about how your competencies fit what the employer is looking for.*		
The 10 most standard competencies used by organizations are: 1. Achievement/Results Orientation. 2. Initiative. 3. Impact and Influence. 4. Customer Service Orientation. 5. Interpersonal Understanding. 6. Organizational Awareness. 7. Analytical Thinking. 8. Conceptual Thinking. 9. Information Seeking. 10. Integrity. This list is merely a starting point. Competencies for a specific organization can be very different based on its culture and goals. Remember, too, that competencies can change as an organization's situation or culture changes.		

Step 3: Understand the Needs of the Employer and the Interviewer

Key Questions and Tasks	Reference Page	Date Completed
Remember that all interviewers are looking for the best candidate for the job. As a candidate, you can help the interviewer by providing information to demonstrate that you are a strong applicant.		
Begin thinking about how you can prove yourself to the interviewer, who will be considering these questions: ☐ *Can you do the job?* ☐ *Will you do the job?* ☐ *How well will you fit with the organization's culture and people?*		
For each competency you have identified as important for the position, be ready to talk about three main elements in your examples: ☐ Situation/Task/Problem. ☐ Action. ☐ Result. Begin to prepare for your interview by outlining these elements for each competency you want to demonstrate.		
Although interviewers are trained to avoid asking illegal questions, this still happens sometimes. *Be prepared to answer illegal questions.* (An "illegal question" is a question about your status in a class that is protected by law, such as race, sex, age, religion, disability, veteran status, color, and ethnicity/national origin.) Try to understand the interviewer's real motivation for asking the question, and respond to the underlying business need that it reflects. Don't take it personally, and don't get angry.		

Key Questions and Tasks	Reference Page	Date Completed
As you develop your answers to expected interview questions, it may be helpful to remember that more organizations are using competency-based interviews for three main reasons: 1. Competency-based interviews reduce the chances that an interviewer will ask an illegal question. 2. Competency-based interviews help the interviewer select candidates with the competencies that the organization needs to be successful. 3. Competency-based interviews help organizations reinforce and strengthen their corporate culture.		

Step 4: Prepare to Answer Competency-Based Interview Questions

Key Questions and Tasks	Reference Page	Date Completed
Competencies provide the interviewer with a target for behavioral questions. To be a successful candidate, you need to focus on the same target: competencies.		
Refine your answers to expected interview questions. Responses to competency-based behavioral questions require examples from your past behavior and experience that will help the interviewer assess how strong you are in the key competency areas needed to be successful in the job.		
To prepare for a competency based interview: ☐ Identify the key competencies for the position. ☐ Think about your strongest accomplishments in each competency area. ☐ Structure your accomplishments using the situation/task/problem, action, and result framework (SAR). ☐ Be concise and complete, and use conversational language in your examples. Use professional terminology that reflects the organization's culture, when appropriate.		
Think about your examples from the interviewer's perspective, and be able to restructure your responses accordingly. For example, if your interviewer is focused on results, begin with the "results" component of your answer, followed by information on the situation and then your actions. Present what is most critical to the employer first.		
Review the following points when you are preparing your competency-based interview responses. ☐ Listen carefully; respond to the question being asked. ☐ Respond using conversational yet professional language. Keep things positive. ☐ Be prepared to answer follow-up questions to provide additional details or competency-related information. ☐ Be prepared to provide supporting details beyond your initial answer.		

Step 5: Prove Your Competencies With Examples

Key Questions and Tasks	Reference Page	Date Completed
Your interview responses should always reflect two key points: ☐ *Modesty is never a virtue in an interview.* ☐ *Being evasive and vague might work for politicians, but it rarely helps in an interview.*		
Refine your SAR responses to make sure you are using the best examples from your personal experience to demonstrate your strength in the relevant competencies for the job. *Hint: If you have difficulty finding strong examples, ask mentors, colleagues, managers, family, and friends for instances in which you demonstrated particular competencies.*		
In competency-based interviews, good responses: ☐ Explain the SAR (situation, action, and result) in enough detail that the interviewer understands what the interviewee is talking about, but not so much detail that the interviewer loses the main point. ☐ Focus on whatever is most critical to the interviewer. ☐ Emphasize the most important or relevant point by talking about it first. ☐ Use conversational and casual, rather than formal or stilted, language, and include professional terminology as appropriate. ☐ Show that you are a smart, savvy employee. ☐ Avoid controversial accomplishments, and always focus on the competencies that are needed to succeed in the organization and the position.		

Key Questions and Tasks	Reference Page	Date Completed
Additional suggestions for preparing strong competency-based responses: ☐ Be direct in your responses. ☐ Talk about what matters most to the interviewer first. ☐ Present yourself in a positive light. Avoid examples that make you look like a victim or a negative thinker. Take ownership of everything that was your responsibility, and don't try to place blame on others, even if they deserve it. ☐ Respond to questions about failures or mistakes by explaining what you learned from the experience that will make you more successful in the future. ☐ Think about your accomplishments from the perspective of different competencies. Almost every situation illustrates more than one competency, depending on which part of the work is emphasized. ☐ If you are well-prepared, you should be able to answer most if not all of the interviewer's questions. If you need to think about an unexpected question (which should happen only once or twice), gather your thoughts so that you can provide a thoughtful response. ☐ Practice your answers. Find someone who is a savvy career coach, manager, or human resources professional to help you fine-tune your answers to the most likely questions. Make sure the person you choose understands competency-based interviewing.		

Step 6: Use Good Nonverbal Communication and Present Yourself as a Strong Candidate

Key Questions and Tasks	Reference Page	Date Completed
Actions speak louder than words. To be perceived as a strong candidate, you need to look and act the part. Focus not just on what you say but on how you say it—just as your interviewer will.		
Think about the competencies required for your target position and the nonverbal cues the interviewer might be looking for with each competency. Remember: nonverbal communication is every kind of communication except the actual words you use.		
To be successful in an interview, in addition to strong competency-based answers, you need to: ☐ Dress appropriately. ☐ Behave appropriately. ☐ Maintain good eye contact. ☐ Have a firm handshake. ☐ Use the right gestures. ☐ Smile at the appropriate times. ☐ Respect your interviewer's personal space. ☐ Respond to your interviewer's nonverbal communication. ☐ Avoid giving mixed messages (in which your nonverbal communication contradicts your words). ☐ Deliver your answers in an organized way. ☐ Converse with the interviewer casually. Remember also to speak clearly and put some energy into your voice. Make sure that your interviewer can hear you, but be careful not to shout.		
Nonverbal cues differ depending on the country and culture in which you are interviewing. Before you interview in a different country, research customs and common business practices to understand what nonverbal communication may be expected in an interview.		
Honesty is, of course, essential in any interview. However, there is a clear different between being brutally honest and being diplomatically honest. Always try to put the best possible spin on your words while remaining truthful.		

Key Questions and Tasks	Reference Page	Date Completed
When your nonverbal communication contradicts your verbal communication, the interviewer will believe the nonverbal message. Avoid giving mixed messages.		
Always look your best on the day of the interview. Lose weight, buy a new outfit, and get a haircut if you need one. If you need advice on your appearance, ask the most polished professional person you know for advice.		

Step 7: Remember Other Interview Tips

Key Questions and Tasks	Reference Page	Date Completed
When you think you're ready, prepare a little more.		
Be prepared to respond to these four common interview questions: *1. Why are you interested in this position?* Focus on how your experience and interests match the organization's needs. *2. Tell me about yourself.* Focus on your work experience, highlighting evidence of the competencies for your target position. *3. What is/are your strength(s)?* Focus on the competency that is most important to the employer (provide two or more examples if asked). *4. What is your biggest weakness?* Focus on a weakness that is not a critical competency for the position. Be diplomatic. If a weakness has already been made evident in the interview (for example, if you are not as concise as you could be), use that as your example.		
Be prepared to discuss any competency gaps—competencies that you cannot prove or that are not your strong points. Talk about how you are compensating for the gap by using your strength in another competency. Or talk about what you have done or plan to do to close that competency gap.		

Key Questions and Tasks	Reference Page	Date Completed
Understand these basic truths about interviewing: ☐ The best-qualified candidate doesn't always get the job. ☐ Schedule interviews for the jobs you are really interested in after you've had a few practice runs for jobs you are less interested in. ☐ The first five minutes of the interview are the most important. ☐ Take a planner or notepad to the interview, but don't use it during the interview. Use it afterward to jot down notes to use in your thank-you notes. ☐ Plan to arrive about five minutes early for an interview. If you arrive any earlier, you may be inconveniencing the interviewer, who has her own schedule to keep. ☐ When responding to the request "Tell me about yourself," confine your answer to about two minutes. ☐ Maintain good eye contact during the interview—but don't stare. ☐ If asked about your previous or current supervisors or employers, be diplomatically honest, and do not talk negatively about them. ☐ If the interviewer asks an illegal question, you must still respond, but try to determine the underlying reason for the question before giving an answer. Respond to the underlying business need. ☐ Be as clear as possible in your answers and your nonverbal communication, because the interviewer's perception is the basis for determining who will be hired. Make your work performance look as good as possible, but don't overstate your accomplishments, and don't lie. Your only job in the interview is to sell yourself, which leads to the next point: **Preparing for the interview is the best use of your time, if you want to be perceived as a serious candidate for the job.**		

Chapter 8

Look at Case Studies for Ideas to Make Your Interviewing Stronger

If I have seen further than others, it is by standing upon the shoulders of giants.

—Sir Isaac Newton

I've been showing you how to get ready for competency-based interviews in the previous chapters, but there are also important lessons that you can learn from other people's experience with these interviews. Read through the case studies included in this chapter and look for examples that remind you of some of your own problems or concerns. I chose these case studies carefully to give you an opportunity to see how I addressed some sticky issues during my coaching session to help them get ready for their interviews—competency-based interviews and more traditional interviews. Many of us have issues in our backgrounds or on our resumes that are difficult to explain in an interview and which may even get us into trouble with the interviewer. By looking at these case studies, you will see examples of how we addressed these kinds of issues and made the candidate's weak areas less obvious.

I believe you are a star, but I know that you may need to be reminded of that fact. You need to feel good about your own competence to do well in any interview. If you don't have that kind of confidence, perhaps you've worked for a manager with a different personality than your own, or one who did not see your strengths or even perceived them in a negative way. At one point in my own career, I worked for a human resources manager who told me I was a terrible writer. His style was simply different from my own—for example, he believed in starting memos with phrases such as "Attached please find...." Now that I've written three books, I have evidence that would make it difficult for him to claim that today. You need to show the interviewer how strong you really are before, during, and after the interview. You can do this!

Now meet the people in our case studies:

- ★ Jessica Gramm, a lawyer working for a prestigious law firm who wanted to work as an in-house corporate attorney.
- ★ Jack Blocker, a human resources vice president who lost his job.
- ★ Dan Marrs, an information technology manager who wanted a promotion within his current company.
- ★ Michael Blakeley, a college senior with minimal work experience, looking for his first job.

All of them had potential, and all of them had issues that could cause an interviewer to pass them over. You might have some similar issues in your background.

Case Study: Attorney

Situation

Jessica Gramm had worked as a litigation attorney for two major New York and Texas law firms, and specialized in handling general litigation and toxic tort cases. She had graduated near the top of her class at a nationally recognized law school in Louisiana and had eight years of experience. She told me she wanted to work as an in-house counsel with a chemical or oil and gas company. For Jessica, the benefits of working in-house included:

- ★ More collaboration and less direct competition with other attorneys.
- ★ The chance to do more preventive work by offering good advice and training managers.
- ★ Less emphasis on marketing, billing hours, and bringing in new clients.
- ★ No concern about making partner.

When I met her, she told me that she had tried for the last two years to make the transition from working as an associate at a law firm to in-house counsel. Although she had interviewed with a few companies, she had not received any offers.

Action

I first worked closely with Jessica to develop a competency-based resume to replace her standard, more traditional resume. As many lawyers do, she was using a resume that covered her credentials, class standing, and the basic facts without giving many details of her accomplishments. We first analyzed an advertisement for a position as a staff attorney for one of the major oil and gas companies that uses competencies to help manage their human resources. We determined the key competencies for the position would likely include:

- ★ Achieves Results.
- ★ Impact and Influence.
- ★ Customer Service.
- ★ Analytical Skills.
- ★ Strategic Agility.
- ★ Team Orientation.

I asked her to think about these competencies and give me an example of a time when she had done high-level work to provide evidence that she was strong in each competency area. Jessica, who had always been a good student, took her homework assignment seriously and had her examples ready the next time we met. We then worked together to develop effective accomplishment statements for her resume, targeting the key competencies. Here are three of the accomplishment statements we used, with the competency or competencies each one illustrated in parentheses at the end:

- ★ Argued and won two Chapter 95 motions for summary judgment in tort cases with pipefitter and insulator as plaintiffs in front of state district judge, 2003–2004 (**Achieves Results**).
- ★ Persuaded partner acting as first chair in trial to avoid using witness who demonstrated memory problems and became increasingly nervous on day before scheduled testimony (**Impact and Influence**).
- ★ Ensured credibility of human resources professional as witness by taking her through direct questions and mock cross-examination to help her know what to expect; recognized for contributing to successful verdict by supporting witness who had considerable difficulty in previous trial (**Achieves Results** and **Customer Service**).

Once we developed credible, targeted accomplishment statements, we worked on her summary section and completed the resume. Within one week, Jessica called to let me know that she had been scheduled for an interview for the staff attorney position with the major oil and gas company. She recognized that interviews at law firms were very different than the interviews she had been through in corporations, and she also knew she had not received an offer in the past. Clearly it was time to try a different approach.

I knew that the company she was interested in worked with competencies, and I told her to expect a typical competency-based interview using behavioral questions targeting those competencies. Some of the work we'd done getting her resume pulled together actually helped her understand the competency-based approach to interviewing. We went through a series of questions targeting the six key competencies we'd identified. I asked her to give me a few examples of times that she:

- ★ Achieved positive results.
- ★ Persuaded someone to do something that benefited a client.
- ★ Went out of her way to help a client.
- ★ Used her analytical skills to benefit a client.
- ★ Developed a good legal strategy.
- ★ Worked well with a team of people.

Like many lawyers, Jessica is articulate, but she needed to polish her style to answer these kinds of questions well. She tended to give very general answers and seemed guarded about what she would share. Many lawyers consider their work to be confidential, but when they refuse to provide details during interviews, interviewers will perceive them as less credible. So the key for the attorney interviewee is to figure out which cases and details *can* be discussed, such as cases that are a matter of public record or no longer sensitive. I coached her to be more specific and to give the information necessary to provide evidence to the interviewers that she was strong in the competencies needed to be successful in the staff attorney role. I also explained how important it is to make sure to include the basics—remember, SAR—in every answer:

- ★ The situation or problem.
- ★ The action you took.
- ★ The result (how it benefitted the organization or client).

Result

Jessica did so well on her first interview that she received an offer. Even with coaching, it is unusual for someone to do that well on their first interview—most of us need more practice. She called after the interview to tell me that the interviewers had asked her the following questions:

- ★ Tell me about a time when you used your judgment to persuade a partner or senior manager to make a different decision in a case.
- ★ Tell me about a time you used complex litigation analysis in a case—what was the result?
- ★ Have you used a litigation strategy? Describe a case where you used a litigation strategy to help you manage the case, and tell us the steps you went through to determine the right litigation strategy to use. What happened?
- ★ Tell us about a time you had to deal with a difficult issue with an employee. How did you handle it? What happened?
- ★ Describe a situation in which you had to deal with a difficult client. How did you handle the situation?
- ★ Tell us about a time when you used your skills and knowledge to help the team. What was your role? What was the outcome or result of your input?

See if you can figure out which competencies the interviewers were targeting with each question. Look at Appendix B for my answers.

Case Study: Human Resources Vice President

Situation

Jack Blocker had a BBA from the University of Michigan and had completed an MBA two years earlier through the University of Phoenix online program. He had worked as a human resources vice president for two medium-sized manufacturing companies and had 30 years of human resources experience. Though he had gained some very good experience in his last role, Jack knew he was a little out of practice with interviewing—or at least doing well in his interviews. His last company had just been acquired by a competitor, and Jack had been doing some consulting work and looking for his next opportunity for about six months when we met. It was very clear Jack was angry about being without a job. He told me, "In all the years I've been working, I've never been treated the way I was by that last CEO."

Action

The first thing Jack and I spent some time talking about was his anger and frustration. I made the decision that Jack could handle my comment: "I think you're lucky. Most people can't say that they've worked 30 years and never been treated badly." He understood my point, thanked me, and told me that he knew I was right. If *you* are angry, for whatever reason, know it *will* come across to the interviewer, and it *will* hurt your chances of being chosen for the position. Even if you think you are smart enough to hide your anger, it will probably still come through during the interview. Before you can do well in any interview, you need to do everything you can to resolve the anger—perhaps even meeting with a mental health professional to get some help in this area.

Even though Jack had worked in human resources, he had worked for companies that were not leading-edge. His last company did not use competency-based interviewing, so when we first started talking about it, he recognized he had a few things to learn. He had read about competencies and had been trained on how to use behavioral interviewing. He recognized that in today's job market, he needed to know how to prepare for a competency-based interview for opportunities at all types of organizations.

We looked at some online advertisements and talked about what it takes to be successful in a high-level human resources position. Jack decided to focus his preparation on these competencies:

- Achieves Results.
- Influence.
- Customer Focus.
- Building Business Partnerships, Relationships, and Teams.
- Consulting.
- Organizational Awareness, Agility, and Savvy.
- Providing Feedback.
- Understanding Business Goals.
- Human Resources Expertise.

Result

Jack decided to work through some of his anger with a mental health professional. Two months later, he worked with me to get ready for his interview. By that time, he had a more positive, can-do attitude, and was not a victim using victim language. He was talking in a way that showed he was taking responsibility for what had happened. It is perfectly normal to be angry when things don't work out between you and an employer, but you can't allow yourself the luxury of staying angry—particularly if you expect someone else to hire you. Just as Jack did, you need to deal with the issues and get over being angry before you can really move on.

Jack went on several interviews during the next three or four months, and did not limit his job search to manufacturing companies, even though that was his background. He eventually received a job offer to be the director of human resources at a medium-sized government contractor in the Washington, D.C. metropolitan area. In professional areas such as human resources, it is often easier to change industries—as Jack did—because a large part of the technical work stays the same, but you will always have an edge if you have experience in that same industry.

During his interview at the government contractor, the CEO and president of the company asked Jack the following questions/directives:

- ★ Describe a time when you had to work especially hard to get a good result. What did you do?
- ★ Tell us about a time when you had to influence a group of people to be able to lead them effectively.
- ★ When you first started with your current employer, what did you do to learn the specific things about the industry that you needed to know to be effective in human resources? How did you decide what was especially important?
- ★ Tell us about one of the most effective business partnerships you've been involved in building. What did you do to help make it so effective? Did you need to overcome any obstacles? Describe what happened.
- ★ Have you been involved with introducing any new ideas or programs into your organization? If so, tell us about the program, and describe the steps you used to gain peoples' acceptance of it.
- ★ Tell us about a time you made a mistake. What did you learn from it?

Case Study: Director, Information Technology

Situation

Dan Marrs was an information technology product development manager working for American Express in St. Louis. I first met him two years ago when he became the first person from a competency-based organization to ask me to help him develop a competency-based resume. At the time I was in the early stages of writing *Competency-Based Resumes*. Dan wanted to stay with American Express—and he wanted a promotion. He knew that a competency-based resume targeting the key competencies for promotional opportunities would help improve the likelihood he would be selected for an interview. He came to me with a list of competencies[1] for the positions within American Express he wanted to post for:

- ★ Creates Innovative Solutions.
- ★ Thinks Analytically.
- ★ Acts Strategically and Globally.
- ★ Drives Results.
- ★ Exceeds Customer Expectations.
- ★ Risk-Taking.
- ★ Acts Decisively.
- ★ Collaborates and Influences Others.
- ★ Demonstrates Integrity.
- ★ Treats People with Respect.
- ★ Manages Performance.
- ★ Develops People.
- ★ Manages Change.

Dan used a competency-based resume to apply for a few positions within the company. (The resume we developed is on pages 46 and 47 of *Competency-Based Resumes*.)

Action

Dan knew that even though he was a strong candidate, other American Express candidates would be equally well qualified for the positions he was interested in. He knew he could not take anything for granted. When an interview was scheduled, he called for help to be as prepared as possible. We focused on the list of competencies he knew were important to be successful in the position he was going to be interviewing for. Candidates who have written a competency-based resume will have an easier time getting ready for a competency-based interview because they have already spent time thinking about what they have done to prove they are strong in each competency area.

I first asked Dan to think of his accomplishments in each competency and have two or three examples in each area. I reminded him that he needed to be able to explain the situation or problem, the action he took, and the result of the action—the benefit to the team or the organization. I listened to his answers and coached him to be:

- ★ Strategic with the examples he picked.
- ★ Concise and powerful with the language he used.
- ★ Professional yet approachable in his nonverbal communication.

Result

He interviewed, did well, and eventually received the promotion.

In most cases, candidates do better in their second or third interviews than in their first one. If the candidate has had a long dry spell of no interviewing, the first interview will help ready him/her for other, more important interviews. Dan interviewed first for another position within the company and was almost selected.

When he found out that another candidate had been chosen, he talked to the key managers and asked for confidential suggestions on what he could do to improve as a candidate. They told him that he wasn't chosen for the position because he didn't have experience managing more than one person and that the other candidate had that experience. Dan actually had managed a group of six employees, but it was before he worked for American Express. Instead of arguing the point, Dan took steps to officially mentor employees and actively looked for opportunities to manage teams within American Express. He stayed professional and kept working hard. Dan also received feedback that the interviewers evaluated him primarily on what he said during the interview. He had worked directly with most of the interview team and felt comfortable that they knew what he had done and what he was capable of doing in the future. In his first interview, Dan hadn't provided the interview team with examples that really showcased his competencies because he assumed they already knew his work on those projects.

Before his second interview, Dan prepared by thinking about the critical competencies for the position—just as he had done for the first opportunity. In addition, he made a conscious effort to answer the competency-based behavioral questions in the interview with his best, highest-level examples and explain them well. He was not going to make the same mistake again of assuming his interviewers would be able to consider examples he did not directly address. For several of the questions, he said he just "spoke as if the interviewers didn't know [him]."

Here are a few of the questions (requests, really) he encountered:

- ★ Tell us about a situation in which you had to take several actions over a period of time and overcome obstacles in order to achieve a business objective.
- ★ Describe a time when you had to identify some key issues in order to guide a group toward the right decision.
- ★ Think of a time when you had many challenging projects with different priorities to manage. Tell us about it.

Managers at companies such as American Express are usually given follow-up questions to help them probe candidates for additional information. Dan knew he could expect follow-up questions, so he had reviewed his background and was prepared to talk about any statistic or detail of a project he used as an example.

Dan was ready to be promoted, and he'd shown his willingness to do what he could to accept the feedback he'd received from managers, and continue to improve his performance at work. He learned from the feedback he had been given, and he thought seriously about his competencies before the next interview. Without a doubt, Dan was prepared for his next interview, and obviously he did well. He received his promotion and became an IT director at American Express.

Case Study: College Graduate, Engineering

Situation

Michael Blakely graduated with a BS in electrical engineering from the University of Illinois, with an additional six classes in computer engineering. He had studied hard and ended up with a 3.57 GPA in an extremely tough engineering program. As many college students do, Michael thought he should focus on his classes and get good grades. He did not think that working as an engineering co-op or during the summers was all that important. So, during his four years in college, he had only worked one summer for a small manufacturing plant in a Chicago suburb. Michael had signed up for several on-campus interviews during the fall semester and had discovered that his limited work experience made him less likely to get selected for interviews than his classmates who had participated in the school's engineering co-op program or had worked in the summer engineering intern programs run by Fortune 500 companies.

Action

When I began working with him, Michael was getting discouraged. He had learned the hard way that having substantial, relevant work experience, either through formal internships, co-op programs, or simply summer jobs, makes a difference with employers. I agreed that it would have been better if he had had more solid work experience at that point—but it was too late to encourage him to get that experience during his last semester in college.

As I talked with him I discovered that even though he had not done the formal engineering internships or co-op program, he had done some work setting up, programming, and maintaining computers for small businesses, individuals, and nonprofit organizations. With this in mind we worked together to rewrite his resume—the competency-based way. I asked him questions about times that he'd demonstrated his competencies in these areas:

- ★ Achieved good results.
- ★ Showed initiative.
- ★ Used his analytical skills.

Then we looked at some online advertisements to see which other competencies companies were looking for in entry-level engineering training programs and other positions. We decided to add:

- ★ Customer service.
- ★ Engineering and computer competencies.
- ★ Planning and organizing.
- ★ Information-seeking.

Working with these seven competencies, I was able to help him develop a much more impressive, competency-based functional resume that included some strong accomplishments that his more traditional resume had not included. In just two examples, he had:

- ★ Worked on a team that won the best engineering project in the mechanical engineering department his senior year.
- ★ Developed a solution to a particularly difficult virus on the computer network for a nonprofit organization working with unemployed people in St. Louis, Missouri.

I encouraged him to continue working with his college job-placement office—but to also start doing a competency-based job search on his own. Before he could actively start a more complete search, however, he received an offer with a medium-sized manufacturing company that his uncle worked for. The human resources manager offered him a contract engineering position at one of their plants for a six-month period. He took the offer even though I encouraged him to keep looking for a full-time, regular position with benefits with a company offering a good training program. Two weeks later, a larger manufacturer announced they planned to acquire the company that had given him the offer. Right before Christmas, Michael was told that the company was going to have to rescind its offer. Michael knew when he called me that it was time to do a much more thorough job search. With his graduation behind him, Michael no longer had the distraction of maintaining a good GPA to keep him from focusing on looking for a job.

When I met with him in early January, we started working on a list of target companies and organizations. In less than one hour we had 30 companies on his list. (It is important to look at this kind of list as a work in progress and be aware of organizations that could be added.) When we put together his list, Michael told me that he'd visited the human resources manager for one of those companies in the hospital with one of his volunteer groups at school. He also knew key managers at five of the targeted organizations because they were family friends or, in one case, the mother of one of his own friends. And I had contacts for him at four more of the companies. So without having to work or think all that hard, Michael found that he had connections at 10 of the organizations he thought he'd be interested in working for. I gave him some ideas about what to say when he talked to his contacts and how to word e-mails and cover letters so that they would be more competency-based.

In addition, Michael still had access to his college placement office and could sign up for interviews during the spring semester. I coached him to go through the list from the school and take advantage of any help the school could offer him. The other thing Michael agreed to do during the next week was to make sure he was listed on Monster.com, Careerbuilder.com, and Dice.com (a site focused on technical professions). He also agreed to check these job sites at least twice each week to see if they had any opportunities he wanted to apply for.

Result

By the end of January, Michael had already been on three interviews and was waiting to see if he was going to get an offer. The interviewers asked him competency-based interview questions, including:

- ★ Tell me about an assignment in school or at work where you needed to have strong analytical skills to do well. How did you plan and organize the work? How did you decide what information you would need?
- ★ Have you worked with a difficult customer? Describe what happened.
- ★ Tell me about the most difficult engineering or computer project you've worked on. Describe what obstacles you ran into, and tell me how you overcame them.

Michael was a very good candidate and had much stronger interpersonal skills than most of engineering students in their early 20s do. In fact, he was just plain likeable—one recruiter who met him described him to me as "charming." He had been a conscientious, hardworking student, and he proved to me that he was willing to take the job search project seriously and work hard at it, too. He received offers from two of the organizations and decided to accept a position at a major hospital in Houston's medical center.

S. Laito
AND WHY WOULD YOU SAY GEENA DAVIS IS YOUR ALL-TIME FAVORITE ACTRESS?...
RESUME
HILLARY CLINTON

Chapter 9

Understand How a Typical Competency-Based Interview Flows

In his book *Blink*, Malcolm Gladwell states that "we learn by example and by direct experience because there are real limits to the adequacy of verbal instruction." In this chapter, I'm going to take this truism to heart and give you an example of how a typical competency-based interview progresses, from start to finish. After all, an interview is a conversation between you and the interviewer(s). To do well, you need to know what to expect.

Most interviews last for about 30 or 40 minutes, unless you are interviewing for a more senior position in an organization. And many organizations still conduct several individual interviews with each candidate, one interviewer after another. The other major exception to the timing is when you are being interviewed by a panel or team; these interviews typically last longer and are being used more frequently. Most interviews can be broken into three parts: the introduction, the body, and the conclusion. We'll be talking about each of these parts, and I'll give you some specific examples to give you a better understanding of how a typical interview progresses.

It is important to realize that interviewers have different levels of competence in conducting and assessing interviews.

Interview—Introduction

At the beginning of the interview, the interviewer will typically meet you in the lobby, introduce himself, shake your hand, and walk with you to the office or conference room. Review the suggestions in Chapter 6 for how you can be perceived as a strong candidate from the very beginning based on your nonverbal communication skills. Remember how critical it is to make a good first impression. If you need to sign any forms, take any tests, or complete any applications as part of the interview process, you will probably be asked to do these things at this time, as well.

Although every organization interviews slightly differently, it is not unusual for the interviewer to open the conversation with an icebreaker, such as:

- ★ Did you have any difficulty finding the office?
- ★ What do you think of the area?
- ★ Would you like some water or coffee?

The interviewer may begin by confirming some facts regarding your background. You may even be asked questions about degrees, dates, or past employers listed on your resume or application—just to confirm details or clarify anything that is unclear. The interviewer may also tell you about the organization's interview process and whom you are scheduled to talk with that day.

Interview—Body

During the body of a competency-based interview, the interviewer asks behavioral questions structured to help him/her determine how strong the candidate is in the competencies critical for success in the position. Usually these questions come from an interview guide approved by key managers in the organization. To help you see how this works, refer to the example in this chapter: a financial sales professional looking for another opportunity. After each answer I've included some coaching tips to help you understand how it could have been even stronger. Because we can't see or hear the candidate's nonverbal communication, the coaching tips are limited to the answers themselves. In the next chapter, you'll have the opportunity to learn from three other professionals: an IT project manager, a consultant, and a financial analyst.

Read through each of these segments carefully. Take note of the responses that you think work well and those that, in your mind, could be improved. Think about how you would respond to these questions yourself. Then review the coaching tips. Hopefully you will get some ideas about what you can say and do to make your next interview more positive and productive. Each interviewee is a strong candidate; as an interviewer, I'd be happy hiring any of them. Of course they also have weaknesses, things they need to work on to learn in order to be more effective. My advice? Read through these examples to get additional tips on what you can do to *nail* that next interview!

Financial Sales Professional

Q: Can you tell me about a project that had a pending deadline that you have worked on and what obstacles you encountered?

A: When I was at Beneficial, I worked on an automated solicitation campaign project. The purpose was to develop an automated system to send out solicitation offers to existing customers. The team had three months to design, test, and implement the system. Time was the biggest obstacle that we had to overcome. The team consisted of branch managers and assistant mangers who did not want to spend a lot of time away from their offices. Another problem was getting the staff of the branches to buy into the automated system.

Coaching

- Overall, a good answer.
- This answer would be stronger if you addressed the underlying question about your results directly. Did your team get the project done by the deadline? Did your management recognize you for completing the project on time or under budget, or for the high quality of the work? What was the bottom-line result of the project?
- Expect to get a follow-up question if you don't address the obvious question about how you overcame the hurdles in your first answer.

Q: How did you overcome these obstacles?

A: I developed a weekly assignment calendar. Each team member was responsible for completing his or her task each week. We would have a conference call once every two weeks and meet twice a month. This system allowed the managers to be able to stay in their offices. In order to get the staff to buy into the system, each manager would ask for input from his or her most senior staff member about the design of the solicitation pieces, and we would share with our staffs how the system would look and work so that the staff felt that they were part of the project.

Coaching

- Good details. This answer would be stronger, though, if you had summarized your main points in a topic sentence at the beginning of the statement. For example: "I did this by making every effort to make sure our team communicated effectively and understood their assignments and goals."

- Good point about getting the staff buy in. By bringing that up, you demonstrated that you understood how to motivate the team.
- Clarify your role. Were you one of the managers or a senior staff member? His answer didn't make that clear.

Q: What was your role in the project?

A: To make sure that we stayed on task and completed the project on time. I also helped with the design of the solicitation pieces.

Coaching

- This answer needs more of an explanation, especially if it was asked before the previous question.
- More details would help you make your role clearer. Did you coordinate the conference calls?

Q: Can you think of a time when you were below your sales goal during the middle of the month or when you missed a sales goal altogether? What did you do to improve your numbers?

A: When I worked as a financial advisor for Fidelity, we were in the middle of an intra-office contest. I was about 10 percent below my goal, and the contest was ending in about 14 business days. I went through my client list and reviewed previous financial plans to see which clients were due for their yearly reviews or if there were parts of the plan that needed to be implemented. I stayed late each night and contacted each client to schedule review appointments. If my client could not make an appointment I asked for a referral that I might be able to contact to schedule for a financial planning session. Using this method allowed me to get my production back on track, and I finished the contest in the top five.

Coaching

- Very good, logical answer, with a few details and specifics that make it credible.
- Remember that your answers need to be conversational—the first part of this answer is just too long. Use shorter sentences to avoid dominating the conversation or just boring the interviewer.

- You could have provided even more details to support how hard you worked to make the goal. How many clients were on your list? How late did you stay each night? Keep in mind that what is late for one person is not always late for another.

Q: Tell me about why you have been successful in sales.

A: I develop a relationship with my clients built on trust and respect. I try to work with my clients using a team approach so that they feel that I have their best interests at heart.

Coaching

- Good introduction, but you should have supported your answer with some specific examples of when you developed client relationships in the past at your former employers (American Express and Fidelity). You will build credibility with the interviewer by citing clients who have referred business to you or given a larger percentage of their overall net worth to you to manage. Remember that most people conducting this type of interview are taught that past behavior is the best predictor of future behavior. So by giving examples of when you have developed productive relationships in the past, you are providing evidence you will be able to continue developing them in the future.

Interview—Conclusion

After the interviewer is done asking the competency-based behavioral interview questions that are included in her interview guide, she will probably ask you if you have any questions for her. If you don't ask questions you'll come across as disinterested in the position, so you should *always* come prepared with questions to ask.

So, what are good questions to ask the interviewer?

1. Questions that demonstrate a genuine interest in the work. The interviewer is talking to you because he or she needs help doing the work.
2. Questions that demonstrate you were listening during the interview.

Ask questions such as these:

- ★ When you think about the other people you've seen working in this position, would you tell me about the employee that you think has been the most successful? What did he or she do in the first year (or six months) to help him/her be so successful? (Note: Pay close attention to the interviewer's answer. It can give you very good information about what the manager is looking for in a good employee.)
- ★ What are your goals for the department? Tell me about them, and why they are important to the organization.
- ★ How have you apportioned the work within the department?
- ★ When you were talking a little earlier, you mentioned ________________ [*bring up something the interviewer told you about the company*]: can you tell me more about that?

You may be thinking that these questions look quite similar to the behavioral interviewing questions that you've been learning about throughout this book—and you'd be right. Congratulations—now you're thinking like a highly competent professional! Here are three reasons you should ask these kinds of questions:

1. They help demonstrate that you want the position and are willing to learn from your future manager.
2. They give the manager an opportunity to talk and give you some good information that may help you understand the position, the people you'll be working with, and the organization's culture better.
3. They show the interviewer that you are smart, current, and savvy.

After you've asked a few questions, see if the interviewer takes back control of the interview. If he doesn't, you might want to say something like this: "I could keep talking with you for a long time and I am having a good time talking with you, but I want to be conscious of your time constraints." See what he says. When one client used this approach during a second interview with a powerful senior vice president, he looked at her, smiled, and said, "Okay, you can ask me two more questions." She did, and she received a job offer three hours later.

Usually, interviewers will tell you what to expect next before you leave the interview. If your interviewer doesn't volunteer this information, tell him that you've been very impressed with everyone you've met and are even more interested in the position than you were before the interview. Ask what the next step is in a polite, professional manner. As well, make sure you have contact information for everyone you've spoken with. The easiest way to get their names, e-mails, mailing addresses, and phone numbers is to ask for their business cards, if they don't automatically give one to you. Finally, when you leave, write down some notes about what was discussed during the interview. Try to do this when you get to your car or when you get home that day. You'll need the notes to write targeted, competency-based thank-you notes.

S. Laib
GIVE ME AN EXAMPLE OF A PROBLEM YOU SOLVED THAT DIDN'T INVOLVE WIRETAPPING...
RESUME
DICK CHENEY

Chapter 10

Learn From Other Interviewees

In the previous chapter you learned how a fairly typical competency-based interview progresses. You read a financial sales professional's answers to some competency-based interview questions, and had the opportunity to learn from the coaching comments. Confucius once said, "By three methods we may learn wisdom: first, by reflection, which is noblest; second, by imitation, which is easiest; and third, by experience, which is bitterest." In this chapter, you're going to be able to gain some wisdom from the interview experiences of three real people: an IT project manager, a compensation and benefits consultant, and a financial analyst.

The examples included in this chapter do not include the introductions or concluding parts of the interview; this is to make it easier for you to focus on the types of questions that are being asked. As you will see, the answers the candidates give are not perfect—few answers ever are. To give you an idea of how the answers could be better, I've included my coaching comments after each one. Read through the questions and answers carefully. Look for examples that you can relate to. Take especial note of an answer, a part of an answer, or a coaching comment that triggers an idea for how you might give better answers in *your* next interview. Remember that our goal here is not perfection but—to paraphrase Confucius—to gain wisdom. At least about interviewing!

IT Project Manager, interviewing for another opportunity within his company

Q: Tell me about a time when you led a team to complete a project. Give an example of a challenge that significantly impacted the project, and describe how you resolved the issue.

A: The project was to lead a team of 10 people to complete installation of new software for Website access to client data. The challenge was that the team consisted of 10 people but several were contract offshore technical resources that were partially allocated to my project and were only dotted-line reporting to me. What made the situation even more difficult were the time difference between Bangalore, India, and the Ft. Lauderdale office, the language differences, and not being trained on the new software.

What I did to mitigate the issues was to pair the contact individuals with a U.S. counterpart. I set up a buddy system to complete specific project task items. The U.S. member was responsible to support the contract partner with needed information or obtain a trained person to support completing the task. Specific weekly conference calls in the evening in the United States to coincide with India's next-day morning were scheduled to track the progress and identify solutions for outstanding issues. Items that required more time to complete that impacted the time line were communicated to management as a risk.

Coaching

- Basically a good answer, with enough details to make the example credible.
- If you realize that one of the most important competencies targeted with this question is **Achieves Results**, you need to focus more on the project results to make this answer even stronger. This is a good example of why understanding the competency-based interview purpose can make a huge difference in the quality of the answer.
- Make sure you use conversational language. Most of us rarely use words such as *mitigate* when we talk—we might say *manage the issues* instead. However, if the organization you are interviewing with commonly uses these kinds of words in conversation, go ahead and use them.
- Take credit for the steps you took to lead the project. Who decided to schedule the weekly calls? Who actually scheduled them?
- Use more active language to describe your role. Who communicated the things that took more time to complete to management? Avoid using passive language.

Q: Give an example of when you had to deliver bad news. Describe how you delivered it and what the response was.

A: The situation was delivery of an enhancement to a large database share by multiple systems without interrupting current operations. The enhancement would facilitate down-line reporting to a business unit that is not an owner of the database. This project is an exception to provide data that would generate $1 million in incremental revenue for the company. The bad news was a higher priority project for the database owners was approved without considering it would delay the "outside" project by a forecasted three months. I had to deliver the news to unreceptive senior management sponsors. I immediately communicated a summary of the potential delay, and what I had done to address the risk. I deliberately said "potential" to communicate the risk without alarming the project sponsors by giving too many details. I immediately escalated to my senior management to advise them of the risk. I also suggested a compromise solution to blend the two projects as an option for my senior management. After negotiation between senior management sponsors, the solution was accepted. The actions of immediate escalation and providing a solution for my management to offer were key to implementing a prompt solution and prevented a major conflict.

Coaching

- Some good information in this answer, but it needs to be more concise and conversational.
- Use active language to describe the SAR—situation, action, and result. Say, "I was told by my manager that a higher priority project had been approved that would cause a delay in several areas—including the project I was working on."
- Try to be consistent with the tenses you use when you are giving your answers.
- Be specific. How many senior management sponsors did you deliver the news to?
- Take credit for the things that you have done and be clear about who did what. Who negotiated between senior management sponsors? Was the fact that you immediately communicated with your senior management and provided a solution, an action? If so, make that clear when you are giving your answer.

Q: Tell us about a time when you demonstrated your ability to effectively communicate to a group. Describe the situation and explain how you knew if you got your message across.

A: There is an annual company tech conference that more than 1,000 clients attend. My responsibility was to present a management information product session. The purpose of the presentation was to convey that the reporting product was simple and flexible enough to support individual users while sophisticated enough to provide global report consolidation. What made it successful was focusing on the benefits of the core product and value via the use of samples of real situations, and conducting the session from the perspective of the audience. In the presentation I overlaid the power of reporting over the true power of the data with comparisons to alternative options. I focused on data management and assumptions, not the tool. The presentation also included data flow charts and report samples. My presentation received the highest rating out of 50 sessions in the conference via attendee surveys. Not only is this presentation style successful for conference clients, but also with internal peers and colleagues in training sessions.

Coaching

- Be more concise and conversational. This whole answer is too wordy.
- Make sure you provide details such as when the event happened.
- The first two sentences would be more effective if reduced to one statement such as, "I was asked to present a Management Information product session at the company's 2004 tech conference." It is probably reasonable to assume that, because this interview is for another position within your company, the interviewers would know about the size of the conference and how important it is to the company.
- Use more *active language*. For example: "I knew that the presentation needed to get across how easy the product is to use for individuals while being sophisticated enough to provide global report consolidations."
- Talk about your result—getting the highest rating at the conference—earlier. That's the most impressive and important part of your answer. Putting this information in the second sentence would give it the emphasis it deserves.
- Good conclusion, but it would be stronger if you phrased it so that it shows what you learned from working on and delivering the presentation. Start the sentence with "I learned that…."

Q: Provide an example of a sound decision you made even though you didn't have as much information as you would have liked.

A: I was managing a project integrating new software that had not been implanted anywhere in the company. There was no experience with installing. The vendor had no experience with how our company wanted to configure and utilize the features. By the second milestone, it became clear the installation would not be completed in one year, and that I would need to ask for additional time and funding to complete the project. Given the urgency to migrate from the old system to the new, senior management needed to understand what the real estimate would be before authorizing the scope change. I asked the technology and servicing team to analyze and assess the phasing of the project. My recommendation was to use an unrelated but similar project as a baseline assumption, and my managers agreed. Once we completed a deep level of analysis, I was able to extrapolate a new time line and scope for the first year delivery with current funding and a reasonable level of risk. Additionally, I presented the consequences of not continuing the project to better balance the investment decision. The outcome was that the phased project approach was accepted.

Coaching

- Basically a good answer.
- Use active verbs. For the second sentence, say, "No one in the company knew anything about installing the software." For the last sentence, use, "The senior managers accepted my recommendation to phase the project in."

Q: Describe how you handled a situation to make sure you stayed on track and completed the tasks needed to drive results.

A: The project was in response to an urgent senior executive request to complete a one-off development enhancement to the product for a high-visibility client to use. I was told I needed to complete the project without interrupting the work on any of my other projects. To be successful and meet my manager's needs, I reviewed the expected deliverables with the client. I needed to understand the detailed information about their needs to then use the information in providing an estimate. As estimates include time, cost, and scope, talking with the client immediately helped me identify that I would need to reset expectations on the delivery time line. An expectation for an early delivery was improperly communicated to client. The requirements needed development of a new process design. I organized a team of subject matter experts and whittled the options down to the optimal option that could be incorporated into an existing project. Although there were numerous issues that required changes in design and subsequently project scope, the project was completed within the year without incremental cost to the client or the existing project the enhancement was incorporated into. Sharing existing resources was key in completing the enhancement. The key tool in contributing to timely delivery was my maintaining a project plan to identify resource availability and task prioritization.

Coaching

- Good example with enough details to be credible. Going through the steps you took, step by step, works well.
- Think through your answer and edit it to eliminate unnecessary words and details. Focus on what is critical for the interviewer to know to understand the example. This answer seems as though it would be a first draft in a paper—you need to be talking in final draft form to be really effective in the interview.
- Start your answer by explaining your role ("I was asked to be the project manager for...).
- Avoid the use of passive voice—use active verbs whenever possible.
- Take credit for the things you and the other people did on the project by being more direct in your statements.
- Avoid using filler words, such as *various* and *numerous*, when you are answering questions. These words don't add anything to the content. You've already shown that there is more than one issue.

Consultant

Q: Tell me about yourself.

A: I'm a problem-solver who thrives on new challenges, and I enjoy following a project through to completion and assessing the team's performance. I prefer working in a team and appreciate the opportunities to share my own ideas and learn from others. I am generally very quick to see connections between parts of a project, or between a project and the areas of the organization that it is intended to impact. I don't mind hard work and long hours, particularly if a project presents the chance to build my knowledge and skills.

Coaching

- Mostly a good answer, but you need to do a better job of answering the question of "Can you do the job?" (covered in Chapter 3).
- It would be a definite plus for you to close with a statement about what you want to do next and why you are ready to do it.
- Try to make the answer a little more conversational, with shorter sentences and slightly more informal language.
- This answer would also be stronger if you led with your profession—"I'm a senior consultant."
- Unless you are confident that a position is 100-percent teamwork, avoid the possible perception that you can't work alone by adding the statement that you are also good working independently when you talk about teams.
- Avoid using ambiguous language—for example, that you "don't mind" something—because it can create the perception that you actually *do* have a problem with it.

Q: Tell me about a time you felt particularly good about the results you were able to get on an assignment.

A: I worked with a partner on an assignment to revamp the salary and incentive compensation program for a major retailing company. Initially, we worked with two of their larger divisions, store chains based in Ohio and Texas. As their management watched our progress, and as we shared our preliminary findings, they were so impressed that they asked us to extend the project timetable to incorporate four additional divisions. Ultimately, we also conducted an executive pay study with personnel at the corporate headquarters.

Coaching

- A very good answer overall.
- Could be even stronger if you started with the bottom line—a statement summarizing the basic answer. For example: "I worked on a

project for major retailing company, and they were so happy with the quality of work that the client added two new divisions to the project after the first month. That meant more than $250,000 in additional consulting fees for the firm."

- Be more specific. Give names of clients and details of projects, including size and scope. Quantify your answers with statistics and consulting fees whenever possible. (It is okay to estimate if you don't have the exact number. Take the time to go through your notes or call a former colleague to verify the information, if possible.)
- Make sure that the language you use is conversational and casual.
- Stay current with your terminology. For example, the word *personnel* is dated; use *employees* instead.

Q: Tell me about a situation in which you had to think outside the box to come up with a good solution.

A: We try to use published surveys to determine appropriate salary levels for organizations, but we've encountered some situations in which the data just doesn't exist. In working with a major telecommunications company, we found several unique jobs that were difficult to place in the company's hierarchy. To determine values for these jobs, we used two approaches. First, we worked with senior management and the managers of these positions to develop very clear job requirements and responsibilities, and we then were able to suggest comparable jobs in the company as well as in other industries. We also used our own sources, including clients, and asked our client contact to provide us with some sources, to obtain salary data at competitive organizations, with the agreement that we would share the data with any organization that contributed to the survey. Through these two avenues, we were able to get more accurate pictures of these jobs, both internally and externally, and client management felt that our results were very credible.

Coaching

- You need to explain why the two approaches you mentioned are really "outside the box." It is hard to tell from your answer. It would seem that most organizations would have some unique jobs, and your consulting group would have figured out a basic approach to use. So give a full explanation; if you can't, consider choosing a different example.

- Be careful about using the word *we* when talking about your work. Always clarify your role. Many interviewers would perceive that as showing that you still think of yourself as part of your past or current employer's team and that you would have trouble making the transition to working for the new manager or employer.
- Make the answer more conversational and use shorter sentences.

Q: Have you managed a project in which it was difficult to meet the deadline or stay within the budget? If so, tell us what happened. How did you address the situation?

A: Yes, I have. We were hired to complete an incentive compensation study for a public utility. Although senior management was involved in the initial meeting, our major contact, the project manager, was at a lower level in the organization. The project manager was constantly trying to extend the scope of the project, asking us to do weekly reports and to cost out many more alternative scenarios than we normally produced. After almost a month of his requests, we asked our relationship manager to contact the senior managers for a progress meeting. When it became clear to the senior managers that we were doing much more than the planned work, they asked us to elaborate on the expected results of our efforts. The end result of the meeting was that the project scope was officially extended, with a revised budget and timetable, so that we could produce some of the additional requested studies and recommendations.

Coaching

- I suspect you missed an opportunity to show the interviewer some evidence of your **Organizational Awareness/Agility** or **Interpersonal Savvy** competencies. Explain why you asked for a progress meeting. Was it because you weren't sure the project manager was keeping her senior management informed? Or was it that you wanted to make sure that the executives wanted the expanded scope of the project and would be willing to pay for it? Either reason shows the interviewer some good things about the way you think and handle yourself professionally.

Q: Describe a time that you had to use your ability to influence a manager to be able to do a good job.

A: I was assigned, along with a project manager, to complete a relatively simple compensation study at a hospital. The project manager had asked to be assigned to a bigger, more-high-profile assignment that was given to another consultant in our group, so he was less than enthusiastic about our project. Once I realized the issue, he and I strategized about ways to complete the project under budget and ahead of schedule, while still maintaining the expected quality and client satisfaction levels. Although we ultimately spent the full budget, the work was completed two weeks ahead of schedule, and our group manager considered that performance in promoting my colleague to a unit manager, which happened about six months after we completed our project.

Coaching

- Very strong example. It not only shows strong influencing skills, but you also are providing evidence of several other competencies, including Achieves Results and Interpersonal Savvy.
- Be more specific—what is relatively simple to one person may not be simple to another.
- Use more conversational language, and be a little more concise. For example, end the last sentence with "...when he promoted my colleague to a unit manager six months later."

Q: Tell us about a time you worked with a difficult person on your team.

A: One of our compensation consultants was well-known for his domineering style in managing projects. He insisted on leading every meeting with the clients and allowed the other team members to talk only rarely. At the same time, he required his team members to prepare all of the materials for each meeting, which he would critique quite candidly in front of the whole project team. In an attempt to help him recognize and change his style, the group managers assigned the two of us as co-leaders of a project with a major aircraft manufacturer. He asked to be reassigned to another project, but the managers refused his request. When it became clear that we would need to work together closely, he gave me his opinion of how the project should be run, and it was clear that he expected me to just accept his ideas. Based on our conversation, I put together a timetable for the project, showing major activities and meetings. I then sat down with him and said that, though I agreed with his concept of how the project should be structured,

I wanted to share more of the workload with him. Although it took a couple of sessions with my chart to get agreement on sharing the load, we did reach what I considered to be an acceptable compromise to his original plan, and our managers were impressed that we both were able to modify our working styles to accommodate each other and our client.

Coaching

- Good choice for your answer. It demonstrates strong interpersonal skills and a matter-of-fact, pragmatic approach to working with a difficult personality.
- It is critical to give an answer to this question. It is just not credible to say that you have never worked with someone difficult. But if you show anger, judgment, or any other negative emotional response in your answers or in your nonverbal communication, the interviewer will perceive you negatively. Be careful. Pick an example showing your wisdom and professional approach to problem-solving.
- Be more conversational with the language you use, and work on being a little more concise and to the point. Ideally, you want to give your answers using "final-draft" language—without redundancies and extra words that don't add to the content.

Financial Analyst with experience in banking and healthcare, interviewing for position with major hospital system

Q: Tell me about your background.

A: I have 15 years' experience in banking as a financial analyst and have worked for the last year in healthcare. Over the years, I have completed studies in banking departments that have included process reengineering and improving operating departments through streamlining processes. I've also most recently managed the customer profitability reporting area, where I have focused on the profitability of our customers and ways to cross-sell and increase revenue.

Coaching

- Be careful not to emphasize the number of years of experience you have. As one manager explained, "Someone can have the same year of experience 15 times." This is especially important for those of us age 35 and older who may be concerned about age discrimination. The important thing to emphasize in your answer is your relevant experience: evidence to prove to the interviewer that you are competent in the key competency areas that are needed for someone to be successful in the position.

- Good job of explaining your overall background concisely. Typically, the answer to this question takes about two minutes to present; most interviewers would view this answer as being too brief.
- The answer would be stronger if you added an explanation of what has motivated you in the past, what your strengths are, what you want to do next, and why you want to do that type of work.

Q: Tell me about a project you worked on in which your analytical skills were critical.

A: As manager of the customer profitability group at BankOne, I had to look at the profitability of the bank's customers and determine which customers were the most profitable and offered the most opportunity for future revenue growth. I also focused on customers with the least revenue potential and initiated exit strategies.

Coaching

- Use language that makes you sound positive. The phrase "I had to look at the profitability" makes you sound like an unwilling victim. Fix the problem by using an action-based verb: "I analyzed the profitability...."
- Give some numbers, statistics, dollars, or some other measurement to quantify the size of the project.
- This answer is okay, but it would be much stronger with more details. How many customers did you review? What process did you use to analyze the information? Did you set up a spreadsheet or database program to help you analyze the information?
- For a much better answer, tell the interviewer what your final recommendation to your manager was, and explain how the bank (or your department) benefited from the analytical work.

Q: Tell me about a time when you had to put in extra effort to get the results you needed at work.

A: This is an ongoing issue. I'm always going the extra mile. If I need to get a report deadline made, I will make it happen by initiating the result needed and making whatever calls I need to get all the pieces to the puzzle complete and on time.

Coaching

- Good general answer, but it would be much better if you brought it down to a specific example. In this case, after giving the general answer, add details such as, "Here's one recent example: Last week, my manager came to my office after lunch and asked me to step in and finish a report for a colleague who had to leave work early when she found out that her fifth grader had broken his leg in a soccer game. The report was due the next morning. I called my colleague on her cell phone, got the details from her, tracked down the information for the monthly report from key department heads, entered the data, and had the report finished and e-mailed to my manager by 8 p.m. that evening."

Q: Have you ever dealt with difficult clients or customers while working at the bank or hospital? Pick a situation and tell me about it.

A: Yes, there are always difficult customers, whether they are internal to the organization or external. One of the most successful strategies is to ask them about ways to improve processes and get their input. By including them in the discussion and valuing their input and finding out what you can improve, many times you win them over. This happens again and again.

Coaching

- Like the previous answer, this one shows your generally good and professional attitude about your customers and your work.
- It would be a much better answer if you backed up your points by giving a specific example to prove what you are saying. Remember to use specific, evidence-based answers whenever possible in order to back up and prove your more general points.
- The interviewer asked you to pick a situation—you needed to do that to do really well on your answer. By not bringing it down to a specific situation, your interviewer may perceive you as lacking in good listening skills. I know you, so I know this isn't true. Next time, just pay a little closer attention and answer every part of every question you are asked.

Q: Tell me about a time when you needed to persuade someone to do things the way you thought they should be done.

A: I had to convince executives that it was very important to develop a strategy focused on calling on bank customers. I persuaded them that it was critical to focus on the customers with the greatest revenue potential and to know which customer segment is the most profitable. Maybe we needed to focus on a different market segment if the customers did not meet the increased profitability goals.

Coaching

- The biggest thing missing here is the outcome: did you convince the executives? How did it benefit the bank?
- Avoid saying that you *had to* do something. Phrase things more positively, using action verbs: "I convinced," "I persuaded."
- Provide more details in your answer (the way you provided them for the executives when you made your case to them). You will always be more credible as a candidate if you can cite numbers and details. This is particularly critical if you are in a profession using quantitative information and details, such as finance, engineering, sales, accounting, or many areas of law.
- Ending your answer with "Maybe we needed to focus on…" would probably cause many interviewers to perceive you as hesitant or unsure of yourself. Try something that is more certain, such as, "After changing the sales strategy, the bank increased profitability by 10 percent the next year."

Chapter 11

Stay Current With Interview Technology and Practices

When *Competency-Based Interviews* first came out, people were talking about smart phones, tablets, iPads, and iPods. As I write this second edition, the Cloud, Geolocation, and contextual-ware computing are becoming more widely known. We've understood the meaning of BYOB for years, but according to Mike Schaffner, an IT director at Cameron, BYOD—bring your own device—is a current IT question, as employees push for using their personal technology at work because it is often more state-of-the art than the technology provided by their employers. Technology continues to change more rapidly than ever, and these changes have impacted how interviews are being done today. In the last five years we've seen an increased use of technology to help make interviews of all kinds more cost efficient, accessible, and effective. While interviews and assessment centers have been used to help select employees in the past, human resources professionals and consultants are now using social media, Skype, Webcams, and virtual assessment centers to help them select the best candidates for positions worldwide.

If you are looking for a new position or getting ready for an interview, you need to be as professional as possible with everything you do, including how you use technology to communicate with the recruiter or potential employer. You may find that employers are including case study questions in their interviews, or you may be interviewing with a consulting firm which uses case study questions as their primary means of assessment. Presenting yourself to a prospective employer used to be pretty simple—you provided your background information in a resume, and when you were contacted you appeared for an interview. Today, you probably present yourself to the world on Facebook, LinkedIn, e-mail, Twitter feeds, and blogs, and your image may not be completely within your control. Even face-to-face interviews have changed—sometimes you're in a group of several prospective employees, and sometimes you are being interviewed by a panel of people representing their employer.

Social Media and the Internet

Are you actively participating in LinkedIn, Facebook, and Twitter? If not, why? Just signing up and friending people or reaching out to expand your networking base may not be good enough to get you the interviews you want today—or enough to create a positive enough impression to cause a recruiter or an employer to decide that you are the best candidate. The most sophisticated social media users realize the power of Facebook, LinkedIn, Twitter, YouTube, and blogs to help create the *right* image of themselves—the image that will motivate an employer to hire them—and to network the competency-based way. It's simply a matter of effective first-impression management, marketing, and personal branding. Here are a few suggestions for how you can make the most of social networking sites:

1. Use a competency-based approach to writing your profiles on LinkedIn and Facebook. Remember that these sites provide an opportunity to position yourself well and increase the chance of getting the interview.
2. Choose your most flattering and most professional photograph. Remember that you can influence someone's first impression of you by selecting that photo carefully. The purpose here is to impress your future employers, business network, and customers, so don't post a photo of you behaving badly or looking unprofessional.
3. Emphasize what you want people to remember by putting it toward the top of your profile. Use persuasive marketing language.
4. Edit what you write to make sure your grammar, spelling, punctuation, and usage are all correct.
5. Target the demographics and educational level of potential employers. Know that Baby Boomers do not expect to get a text message from a candidate—unless, of course, they've asked you to communicate that way.

If you have been resisting signing up for one of these sites because you value your privacy, please know that recruiters and employers will have a harder time finding you, and you may be skipped over for positions. Recruiters and hiring managers now routinely check LinkedIn profiles; if you don't have one, or if it is very minimal, you may seem outdated or even furtive.

Learn how to use the social media sites to help you build your image online. Good places to start? Enter phrases such as *better LinkedIn (or Facebook) profiles* on Google or Bing and read current online articles. Libraries, colleges and universities now have classes on using social media and writing profiles, and there are also classes and Webinars available online. Check with nonprofit organizations helping people looking for employment.

Expect to be Googled and checked out online before the interview, and be prepared to answer questions about *anything* you may have written about in your profiles or blog. You should Google yourself every two or three months so that you know what a recruiter or potential employer is going to see. Pay special attention to what is on the first two or three Google pages because it is unlikely that people would look much further. I heard one story from an IT manager about how, when he Googled the name of a candidate his supervisor wanted to hire, he came across the profile of a sex offender in Florida. He checked with the supervisor and was relieved to learn that the potential employee was not, in fact, the sex offender.

Know that you can manage your Internet presence but you cannot totally control it. One of my books received a one-star rating on Amazon because it was delivered late to a reader. I e-mailed Amazon repeatedly but they never took the rating off, even though it was truly unfair because the one-star rating had nothing to do with the content of the book. Eventually there were enough newer ratings that the unfair rating was moved further down the page. If there is any negative content on the Internet about you, consider writing a blog with enough postings to cause the less desirable item to drop off the first Google page. Remember to Google interviewers and check them out on the social media sites, too. You may learn some interesting things about their backgrounds that will help you establish a connection with them in the interview. Depending on their personal settings they may be able to tell that you looked at their profile, so you may choose to have yourself show up as an "Anonymous LinkedIn User" or have a friend look them up for you.

Skype and Webcams

Arthur C. Clarke, author of *2001: A Space Odyssey*, said, "Any sufficiently advanced technology is indistinguishable from magic."[1] Some of us may use Wifi to look things up on the Internet but cannot begin to explain why it works. Add Skype to that same list. I'm convinced it's magic. In the last few years, Skype has become a major way for professionals all around the world to text message and make long distance calls. Some of us living in the United States have not been as quick to pick up on this technology. One possible explanation is that the telephone and videoconferencing infrastructure in the States is so reliable that we haven't needed to turn to Skype as quickly. But as we do business and network with people worldwide, Skyping is becoming more and more expected.

We're seeing more recruiters and human resources professionals using Skype for interviews because it allows the recruiter to see the candidate while eliminating the cost of travel and long distance calls. I read one discussion about this trend on the LinkedIn HR site, and it became clear that one major use is to replace the initial screening interview. One vice president of human resources wrote that he uses Skype extensively because it helps with scheduling contingencies. He also indicated that some of the positions actually require candidates to communicate with interviewers using Skype, which then enables the company to assess how candidates perform using Skype for training, teaching, or consulting. He did cite one negative "side effect," however—that interviewees seem to be approaching these kinds of interviews much less seriously than they have in the past.

Getting comfortable with the idea of being interviewed via Skype or in a videoconference call is especially critical if you are interested in a position that is based in a different part of the world or requires the use of these kinds of tools. Some examples? Consultants, engineers, and professors or trainers teaching online courses. According to one of my clients, Skype is now being used by admissions officers to interview candidates from outside their geographic areas for MBA and other graduate programs. If you can, try to have an on-campus interview first, but if that is not practical, ask for a Skype interview or an interview with an alum in your area.

If you are from one of the older generations, please realize that it is especially important to stay current with the technology, including Skype and Webcams, being used by recruiters today. We all tend to expect Generation Y (or Millenials) to be using the latest technology, but if you are a Baby Boomer, you may be hurting yourself in the job market if you resist or ignore these changes.

When you have a Skype or videoconference interview:

- Take it just as seriously as you would an in-person interview, and *prepare.*
- Dress professionally, just as you would if you were being interviewed in person or on a TV program—no busy patterns or stripes that are distracting to the interviewer. This is especially true if your Webcam is low resolution.
- Consider key competencies for the position and make sure your nonverbal communication is consistent with these competencies. Look and act the part. (Review Chapter 6 for more pointers.)
- Look at the camera, not at the computer screen or your notes.
- Point the camera at a neutral background, preferably one that is a solid color.
- Before the interview, test your camera and microphone by Skyping with a friend. Check the lighting to make sure that you're not creating unflattering shadows.
- Know that there may be a lag immediately after someone speaks. Don't let these kinds of technological problems bother you—it is an opportunity to show your professionalism. Shift your attitude to expect a technology problem, and then be pleasantly surprised if you don't have one.
- Be careful to eliminate background noise, especially if you are Skyping from home.

Assessment Centers and Virtual Assessment Centers

Organizations have worked with assessment centers for many years to help them evaluate candidates for hiring and promotion, and for lateral moves into entirely different roles. Matthew Tonken, vice president of Talent Management Solutions for the consulting firm Sandra Hartog & Associates explained, "Assessment centers use a set of exercises, such as in-baskets, role plays, psychometric tests, and interviews, designed to evaluate a defined set of competencies. The use of multiple exercises and multiple assessors reduces bias and increases the reliability of the process." Candidates are evaluated by trained line managers, human resources professionals, or psychologists to determine whom should be recommended for an offer. So what are they looking for? In an online article titled

"The Assessment Center Method, Application, and Technologies" by William C. Byham at Development Dimensions International, "Simulations are designed to bring out behavior relevant to the most important aspects of the position or level for which the assessees are being considered." In other words, candidates are being evaluated for behaviors and actions demonstrating strength in the key competency areas the organization has identified for someone in this position to be successful in the future.

The Internet, Skype, Webcams, and videoconferencing have simply changed the logistics of putting together what Sandra Hartog & Associates calls *virtual assessment centers* (VACs) and made them significantly less expensive to conduct. As Matthew Tonken said, "An organizational psychologist located in New York can collaborate with line managers in London to assess individuals in Hong Kong, for an organization based in Geneva, Switzerland." Using the Internet and Skype, conducting an assessment center in another part of the world is also much less expensive than it used to be because travel and telephone costs are eliminated. Whether you're dealing with a regular assessment center, a virtual assessment center, or a psychological test, my best advice is *don't try to game the system*. If your personality really isn't a fit for the position, you won't be successful in it over the long term anyway, and you certainly won't be happy. I would encourage you to be aware of the competencies for the position and the organizational values. Get a good night's sleep before participating in any interview or assessment center activity. Make it a good day, and use your better-than-average social skills that demonstrate strong emotional intelligence.

Communication and Technology

Recruiters and hiring managers have used e-mail as a way to communicate with candidates for several years. Candidates still need to remember to check their e-mail at least twice a day, and, when communicating with potential employers, use complete sentences, proper punctuation, and no internet shorthand or cutesy emoticons. What's new is that we're seeing more organizations include a timed written essay test before the actual interview to help them screen candidates based on their answers to the questions and their ability to write effectively under pressure. Typically, the test is e-mailed to the candidate with instructions about when to open the attachment and how long to work on the test. Make sure that your computer, software and Internet connection are working well, because you don't want your computer to crash when you really need it. Have a Plan B in mind in case you have a problem. Examples of questions that might be included are covered in the section on case-study interview questions later in this chapter.

Another important thing to remember is that e-mails are being used more frequently in legal cases. Be careful not to put anything in an e-mail that you might regret later. Even if you delete a message, a computer forensics specialist could probably still find it, so it's better to just avoid writing it in the first place. Be careful to send emails to potential employers between 6 a.m. and midnight, because e-mails are date- and time-stamped, and you do not want an interviewer to notice that you were awake when most people sleep. Communicate with recruiters, human resources professionals, and hiring managers professionally, and consider their communication needs as more important than your own. For any of us interviewing with someone from a different generation, respond to the recruiter or interviewer using the same channel they used with you—that is, if you received an e-mail, respond using e-mail. Don't consider texting unless the recruiter or potential employer texts you first.

Answering Case-Study Interview Questions

One of the more recent trends is the increasing use of case-study questions during interviews. Consulting and venture capital firms such as McKinsey and Bain have used the case-study interview approach for many years, but their use has spread as consultants from these types of firms have moved into other positions in corporations or other organizations. Case studies have been used in business schools for more than 100 years—anyone who has an MBA will remember them well. Such case studies are typically historical descriptions of actual business situations, in which information is presented about a firm's products, markets, competition, financial structure, sales volume, management, employees, and other factors affecting the firm's success.[2] This approach is also used at law firms and in legal departments to help interviewers evaluate how well candidates think on their feet, present cases, and respond to challenges. Fortunately a case-study question during an interview is usually shorter than the several pages many MBAs will remember analyzing and writing about. So how does it work?

The Website Caseinterview.com includes some good examples of cases that have been included in actual interviews at major consulting firms. Here is one question, identified as a McKinsey case:

> *Your client is a gas station and the market is so competitive that they make no money on gasoline sales. All the profit is in convenience store sales. What is the profit maximizing way to lay out the convenience store and why?*

Here's another example from one of my clients of a case-study question used to screen candidates for an administrative manager position at a large nonprofit:

> *The executive director at the local chapter wants to assess whether the organization is structured in the best possible way. As a member of the senior management team and advisor to the executive director on all administrative issues, you have been requested to provide your input. Describe how you would go about this exercise. Make sure you clearly identify the areas you would focus on, tools you would use to help with your analysis, and principles that you would consider before making your final recommendation.*

This type of question can be included in the interview or used as a way to screen candidates and assess their answers and writing skills in a timed, written test. In a written test, the candidate is typically given two to four questions, and one to three hours to answer the questions online.

What is the interviewer looking for? When I spoke with Marc Cosentino, author of *Case in Point: Complete Interview Case Preparation*, president of CaseQuestions.com, and the former associate director of career services at Harvard, he explained that some of the key things interviewers look for are "what you take into consideration, the logic of your thought and how well you can articulate it. When the interviewer challenges you, can you defend your answer without getting defensive? Did you think it through?" He explained, "There is a lot of math in these questions and you can't use a calculator. They are testing not to see if you can multiply or divide, but to see if you think before you speak." One of the reasons interviewers might use a case-study question is because if you are given the position, you might be asked similar questions by senior managers and clients. How quickly can you answer questions that require analysis and strong quantitative skills? Consider practicing your responses to questions such as these with a professional who has done work in this area. If you are asked this type of question, add the **competency-based interview** spin to the beginning or the end of your answer to illustrate that you have real-world experience related to the key points you are making. Whenever possible, relate the situation to something you have done that shows a competency-based accomplishment. For example, answer the convenience store question and then add the following:

"I actually worked on a project like this when I was with Amoco. My team researched best practices at the five major competitors in the region, and recommended following the layout used by a major competitor—to make sure that the impulse purchases were near the front of the store, near the cash register. If I worked on that project today, however, I'd change my approach to broaden the types of convenience stores we looked at to include major independent service stations, those outside the region and even internationally, and more traditional convenience stores that are not part of a gas station, for a more innovative and comprehensive idea of best practices."

Here's the evidence that this is good advice. After writing this section, I coached the client from the large nonprofit for another position within his organization. One of the questions included in the most current written test portion of the selection process:

> *As the chief external officer, you will be a key advisor to the chief executive officer. Drawing on your career and experience for concrete examples, please describe how you identify challenges, come up with creative solutions, and evaluate your own performance in advising senior leadership and board members.*

Remember, when answering case-study or hypothetical interview questions, *your answer will be stronger if you include examples from your past experience*.

Technology Changes

To be considered a strong candidate you must do well in a variety of interview situations. The good news is that while the situations may have changed, the ways to stand out are still the same—know who you are and what your competencies are, and make sure that you present this information in the best possible way. We've seen the kind of change technology brings. If you look at the changes in the logistics of competency-based interviewing in the last five years, it is clear that technology is having a major effect on interview practices. So here's the challenge. Technology is going to keep changing, faster and faster, and it will continue to change some of the ways we conduct competency-based interviews. Connect with me on LinkedIn, and let me know about the changes *you're* seeing.

Key Points for Chapter 13

Technology continues to change more rapidly than ever, and so do competency-based interview practices.

Key Questions	Answers
How has technology changed competency-based interviews?	Social media, Skype, Webcams, and virtual assessment centers are giving employers more options in the recruiting, interviewing, and selection of employees.
Why should you participate in social media?	Recruiters and potential employers can find you more easily.
Why is it important to use social media in a sophisticated way?	Having well-written LinkedIn and Facebook profiles is an opportunity to manage your image and market yourself. You want to help create the *right* image of yourself on the Internet—the image that will motivate an employer to hire you. It's simply effective first impression management, marketing, and personal branding.
What should you keep in mind when developing your profiles, writing blogs or Twitter tweets, or trying to ensure that future employers will be impressed with what they learn about you online?	• Use a competency-based approach to write your profiles on LinkedIn and Facebook. These sites provide an opportunity to position yourself well and increase the chance of getting the interview. • Choose a flattering, professional-looking photograph. The purpose is to impress your future employers, business network, and customers, so don't consider posting a photo of yourself looking anything other than your best. • Emphasize what you want people to remember by listing it first. Use persuasive marketing language. • Edit for grammar, spelling, punctuation, and usage. • Demonstrate the educational level required by potential employers, and use professional language.

Key Questions	Answers
Why should you make sure your LinkedIn profile in particular is up-to-date and markets your background effectively?	Recruiters and hiring managers routinely check LinkedIn profiles; if you don't have one or if it is very minimal, it can look as though you are trying to hide something.
How can you improve how you use social media or write better online profiles?	Read current online articles or take traditional or online classes/Webinars at libraries, colleges, and universities on social media and writing profiles. Check with nonprofit organizations that help people looking for employment.
Why is it important to know what is being said about you on the Internet?	Because it could come up in the interview. Expect to be Googled before the interview, and be prepared to answer questions about *anything* you may have written about in your profiles or blog. Google yourself every few months so that you know what an employer is going to see. Pay extra attention to what is on the first two or three Google pages.
What can you learn about the interviewer online?	Google interviewers and check them out on social media sites. Look for a connection or a commonality that could help you in the interview. Be careful not to leave a major footprint—they may be able to tell you looked at their LinkedIn page.
How are recruiters using Skype?	More recruiters, human resources professionals, and graduate admissions professionals are using Skype for interviews because it allows the interviewer to see the candidate while eliminating the cost of travel and long distance calls.
Who may be asked to have a Skype interview?	Anyone, but it is especially likely if you are interested in a position based in a different part of the world or which requires the use of Skype and videoconferencing tools. Consultants, engineers, and professors or trainers teaching online courses may be expected to do part of their interview using Skype.

Key Questions	Answers
What can you do to increase your chance of success in a Skype interview?	◆ Take it seriously. Prepare. ◆ Dress professionally—no busy patterns or stripes that would distract the interviewer. This is especially true if your Webcam is low resolution. ◆ Consider key competencies for the position and make sure your nonverbal communication is consistent with these competencies. Look and act the part; review Chapter 6 for more pointers. ◆ Look at the camera, not at the computer screen or your notes. ◆ Point the camera at a neutral background, preferably one that is a solid color. ◆ Test your camera and microphone before the interview by Skyping with a friend. Check the lighting to make sure that you're not creating unflattering shadows. ◆ Anticipate technology problems, such as a lag after someone speaks. Don't let these problems bother you—it is an opportunity to show your professionalism. Expect a technology problem, and be pleasantly surprised if you don't have one. ◆ Be careful to eliminate background noise, especially if you are Skyping from home.
What are assessment centers?	This is a formal method to evaluate candidates for hiring or promotion, or for consideration for a different role. It uses job-related simulations (in-basket exercises, group discussions, interview simulations, fact-finding or problem-solving exercises, presentations, and writing assignments), interviews, and psychological tests.
What are the line managers, human resources professionals, and psychologists evaluating candidates in an assessment center looking for?	Candidates are being evaluated for behaviors and actions demonstrating strengths in the key competency areas the organization has identified that someone in this position needs to be successful in the future.

Key Questions	Answers
What are virtual assessment centers?	Assessment centers conducted remotely using Skype, Webcams, or videoconferencing software. Conducting an assessment center in another part of the world is much less expensive than it used to be because travel and telephone costs are eliminated.
What's the best advice if you are asked to participate in an assessment center process?	◆ Don't try to game the system. If your personality is not a fit for the position, you won't be successful in it long term, and you won't be happy. ◆ Be aware of the competencies for the position and the organization's values. ◆ Get a good night's sleep before participating in any interview or assessment center activity. ◆ Make it a good day, and use your better-than-average social skills that demonstrate your strong emotional intelligence.
What should you remember about e-mail when you are interviewing for new positions?	◆ Check your e-mail at least twice a day, and, when communicating with potential employers, use complete sentences, proper punctuation, and no internet shorthand or emoticons. ◆ E-mails are being used more often in legal cases. Be careful not to put anything in an e-mail that you might regret later, because a computer forensics specialist will likely be able to find it, even if you delete it. ◆ Send e-mails between 6 a.m. and midnight; e-mails are date- and time-stamped, and the interviewer may notice you are awake at a time when most people are asleep.
What are some other things to consider when working with technology in an interview?	Make sure that your computer, software, and Internet connection are working well, because you don't want your computer to crash when you really need it. Have Plan B in mind in case you have a problem. If you interview with someone from a different generation, respond to the recruiter or interviewer using the same channel they used with you—for example, if you received an e-mail, respond using e-mail. Don't text unless the recruiter or potential employer texts you first.

Key Questions	Answers
What is a case-study interview question?	A question describing a situation and asking you to solve a problem or recommend solutions. These questions can vary in complexity based on the position you are interviewing for, and they can be included as part of a competency-based interview or as a stand-alone, case-study interview. One of the reasons interviewers use case-study questions is that if you are offered the position, you might be asked similar questions by senior managers and clients.
What is the interviewer listening for when he/she evaluates your answer to a case-study interview question?	◆ How logical are you? Are you able to answer questions well on your feet in a professional, non-defensive way? ◆ How quickly can you answer questions that require strong quantitative skills and some analysis? Consider adding the competency-based interview spin to the beginning or the end of your answer to illustrate that you have real-world experience related to the key points you are making. Whenever possible, relate the situation to something you have done that shows a competency-based accomplishment.

Chapter 12

Develop Global Competencies for the Future

Peanuts creator and cartoonist Charles M. Schultz said, "Don't worry about the world coming to an end today. It is already tomorrow in Australia." When I conducted competency-based interview training in Guam at the end of 2011, stores were selling t-shirts with the slogan, "Guam USA—Where America's day begins." It is easy to see that both examples are from an American perspective. My Australian friends and readers could just as easily say that America is always going to be a day behind. Americans and Europeans will *never* catch up with the Australians or Asians as long as the International Dateline doesn't move. At least we know that with the internet and CNN, we all have a chance to learn major international news at the same time, or on a fairly real-time basis.

Corporations doing business internationally have always had to make difficult decisions about the best way to be organized. Should they set up a foreign subsidiary or do a joint venture with a company in the host country? Are key decisions made at corporate headquarters or are they made at the company's subsidiary or division based in another country? International nonprofits, hospitals, and schools deal with many of these same issues when they decide to open an office, clinic, or campus in another country. This trend is growing. For example, Northwestern University, my alma mater, decided to establish its first overseas campus in Doha after being approached by the Qatar Foundation for Education, Science, and Community Development in 2006.[1]

In addition to making decisions about how international parts of an organization should be structured, organization leaders also have to decide whether to use the same competencies worldwide or define the competencies differently based on the differences from culture to culture, country to country. Do they want one set of competencies worldwide? Are organization leaders expected to demonstrate the same key leadership competencies wherever they work, while competencies for employees may be treated differently by location? Do they believe there are cultural differences that would make employees behave differently in Japan than in the United States? Do they choose to use the same competencies but adjust the behavioral indicators for different countries or cultures?

Max Underhill is the Managing Director for Maxumise, a regional human capital management company based in Sydney, Australia. He told me he typically recommends that organizations use the same competency framework for their employees throughout the world, and that he believes that most organizations typically use the same set of leadership competencies worldwide. Dick Gerlach, a senior consultant with Workitect, a firm that specializes in developing competency models, agrees with him. He's seen two of his clients, a global cosmetics firm and an international engineering firm, make the decision to use one set of leadership competencies worldwide.

François Ducharme, Managing Director of Hay Group's office in Ottawa, Canada, has a slightly different perspective. He said that they are "moving away from the one-size-fits-all model," and that generally, the behaviors used to demonstrate competencies may be different from culture to culture and from leadership role to leadership role. For example, in the United States, someone with strong customer service skills might provide a major client with his personal cell phone number but this is much less likely to happen in Europe or Canada where privacy is very important. Organizations may have different types of leadership roles that require different competencies for success.

He told me that even translating competencies from one language to another includes some subtleties, such as word connotation, that need to be considered. To illustrate the point, Francois told me that one of the words for conflict in French, *conflit*, often means *interpersonal problem*, and that is the more widely used definition.

One major international nonprofit, headquartered in Switzerland, has employees working in more than 100 countries worldwide. Their global competencies, which are posted online, include:

1. Communication in a Credible and Effective Way
2. Knowing and Managing Yourself
3. Producing Results

4. Moving Forward in a Changing Environment
5. Fostering Integration and Teamwork
6. Respecting and Promoting Individual and Cultural Differences
7. Setting an Example

Please notice that the competencies they've listed are very similar to the competencies at Johnson and Johnson and many of the organizations we've already discussed. You can find other examples of international competencies on the internet by Googling the name of an organization and words like *competencies* or *global competencies*.

In this chapter, we're going to look at global and intercultural competencies that have been defined for people working in international positions. They may be consultants or engineers working on projects in other countries with different cultures, or they may be interviewing for positions with international nonprofits like the United Nations or NATO. Later we'll focus on some specific competency-based interview practices in Canada and India, to give you some perspective about how competency-based interviewing can be different depending on the country in which you are interviewing or where the organization is based.

Intercultural Competencies

In addition to looking at the typical competencies used by organizations with employees living and working throughout the world, some organizations look at *intercultural competency*, which has been generally defined as "the ability to function effectively in another culture."[2] If you are going to be interviewed for a position as a country manager in a different country for an energy company, you need to be able to be bicultural, and if possible, bilingual quickly.

Michael Stevens is a partner in the Kozai Group, a consulting firm of professors focused on intercultural research and training, and a management professor and department chair at Weber State University in Ogden, Utah. He talked about how "the difference in domestic and global leadership competencies is one of degree. With a global organization, managing people can become more complicated based on culture." He said, for example, that in terms of managing people, the difference between managing people in Seattle, Washington in the United States and Vancouver, British Columbia in Canada may not be as great as the difference between Seattle, Washington, and Birmingham, Alabama—even though they are part of the same country. In other words, according to Mike Stevens, "The intercultural leadership challenges with domestic diversity may be just as challenging as global leadership."

In an article published in *The Journal of Managerial Psychology*, Mike Stevens and three colleagues identified three major intercultural competencies: *perception management*, *relationship management* and *self-management*.[3] Like many of the current competency models, these major intercultural competency factors have competencies listed under them.

Intercultural Competencies[4]		
Perception Management	**Relationship Management**	**Self-Management**
Non-judgmentalness	Relationship Interest	Optimism
Inquisitiveness	Interpersonal Engagement	Self-Confidence
Tolerance of Ambiguity	Emotional Sensitivity	Self-Identity
Cosmopolitanism	Social Flexibility	Emotional Resilience
Interest Flexibility	Self-Awareness	Non-Stress Tendency
Stress Management		

If you have an interview for a position which is based in another culture or requires you to interact with people from other cultures, start thinking about what you've done in the past that provides evidence you have been successful in similar situations. Expect competency-based interview questions targeting these types of competencies.

For example, let's think about a competency-based interview question that could be asked to target the competency, **Cosmopolitanism**. According to the article, cosmopolitanism is "a natural interest in and curiosity about different countries and cultures."[5] Here's one question: *Tell me what you did to get ready for your business trip to Rio de Janiero.* This could be followed up with additional or probing questions, such as: *What did you do in your free time while you were there? What would you do differently if you have another opportunity to go there?*

From a coaching perspective, if you are interested in working in another country or culture, please know that a tendency to play it safe when you are traveling and find restaurants or activities available to you at home does not demonstrate **Cosmopolitanism**. I know one professional, for example, who looks for an Olive Garden restaurant whenever he goes to another city because he knows that the food will be good there. Even though I saw the McDonald's restaurant when I was in Singapore, I didn't stop there—I tried as much of the local food as I could, including chili crab and durian.

This reluctance of some people to adapt or change also may be part of the intercultural competency, **Social Flexibility**. As Mike Stevens told me, "Some of the cutting-edge researchers in the intercultural competency area are recognizing that personality traits are immutable—extremely difficult to change." One example we talked about was flexibility, because even if you trained someone to try to modify their rigid approach, it probably makes better business sense for an organization to choose another candidate for the position who has a more flexible approach and personality.

Another example would involve the competency, **Non-judgmentalness**. The definition used in the article is "the extent to which one is inclined to withhold or suspend judgment about persons or situations or behaviors that are new or unfamiliar."[6] Here's a question that might be asked: *Give me an example of when you've had an experience with people from another culture doing something unusual or odd.* The interviewer would be listening for negative language and paying attention to any nonverbal communication that contradicted the words the candidate used.

One of my clients who was born and raised in the United States comes from a family that immigrated to the United States during the Cuban Revolution in the 1950s. He has been successful as a country manager in several Latin American countries because he's fluent in Spanish, and he adapted to each culture quickly because of his work experience in Latin America and his strong intercultural competencies. Even though the Cuban culture he's been exposed to at home differs from the cultures of Mexico and countries in Central and South America, he is able to quickly identify the commonalities, which demonstrates the competency, **Interest Flexibility**, another **Perception Management** competency.

From country to country, from culture to culture, there can be some differences in which competencies are emphasized, the behavior that demonstrates these competencies, and how competency-based interviews are administered. I chose to focus on two very different countries, Canada and India, to give you an opportunity to see some of the interesting ways competencies and competency-based interviews are approached around the globe, and what you might need to consider if you have an interview in one of these countries. Both are very diverse countries, and their organizations demonstrate a range of sophistication about competencies.

Canada

As I interviewed consultants for *Competency-Based Resumes*, the first edition of *Competency-Based Interviews*, and *Competency-Based Performance Reviews*, I kept hearing how good some of the competency work in Canada was. After *Competency-Based Interviews* was first published, I was contacted by a student from Dalhousie University in Halifax who was applying for medical school in Canada, where they routinely use competency-based interviews in admissions. I was also called by a member of the Royal Canadian Mounted Police, or "The Mounties," to help him get ready for a competency-based interview. So when I knew I was going to be including a chapter focusing on international competency-based interviews, it was obvious—I needed to look north.

The Canadian federal government is one of the largest employers in Canada and has been working with competencies for close to fifty years. According to François Ducharme, the emphasis on competencies dates back to the Public Service Employment Act in Canada which became law in 1967. The key parts of the law focused on "merit, non-partisanship, fairness, access, transparency and representativeness."[7] In Canada, "people who are hired and promoted in the public service must possess certain competencies, skills, and experience."[8]

The emphasis on transparency is evident when you look at the material available online. The Canada Revenue Agency has their behavioral and technical competencies listed, and they include behaviorally anchored rating scales providing descriptions of the expected behaviors.[9] According to François Ducharme, when you work within the Canadian Revenue Agency, you know the competencies for your own position, and you have the ability to easily access the competencies identified for other positions you may be interested in for the future. Very detailed instructions about their Targeted Behavioral Event Interviews are available online.[10] For example, they make it clear that they are

> "...asking you to talk about yourself, so the Competency Consultant will be listening for 'I' statements—'I said,' 'I did,' etc. This will help him/her to clearly understand your role in the event you are describing. Please note that the Competency Consultant cannot give you credit for a behaviour that cannot be clearly associated with you, so please avoid using 'we' when describing your own behaviours."[11]

One obvious difference from the United States—the way they spell behavior!

The agency has people trained to interview candidates and assess the level of competencies demonstrated in the examples candidates use in their answers to the interview questions. In some cases, according to François Ducharme, the candidates are given the list of questions before the actual interview so they have an opportunity to think about how they want to answer the question and which examples are the most relevant to the new position.

One of the concerns for many managers throughout the world is that candidates will exaggerate their accomplishments, or even lie about them, during the interview. At The Canada Revenue Agency, candidates are told they should not lie, and they are asked to sign an agreement giving the agency the right to validate or check the examples that the candidate uses in the interview. Candidates need to be prepared to provide the interviewers with a list of people who can confirm the details of their examples and the specific contribution made by the individual if they were part of a larger project or team. The system is so sophisticated that "indicators of embellishment" have been identified. When too many "indicators of embellishment" are used during the interview, it triggers a validation check.

If you are interviewing in Canada with the federal government or many of the other employers who have a similar competency-based interviewing process, make sure you have reviewed their information about their competencies and their interviewing process. Remember that it is simply prudent to think about your strongest, most relevant accomplishments for each competency the employer has identified for the position. By now, you should realize that this advice applies outside of Canada, too.

India

India is currently the second most populous country in the world and is expected to overtake China to have the world's largest population by 2025. It is generally recognized as having one of the fastest growing economies in the world, and this strong business growth creates some challenges and opportunities for international companies and Indian-based companies.[12]

Hay Group has an interesting white paper, *The Indian CEO: A Portrait of Excellence*, on its Website, which makes the point that "to succeed in India, international executives have to view the business landscape from an Indian perspective, recognizing that business is seen as a social good."[13] The firm's research showed that Indian CEOs are focused on growth and have strengths in key competencies: socially responsible business acumen, team leadership, inner strength, and the ability to manage external stakeholders. As compared to the best CEOs from other countries, Indian CEOs also have "higher levels of adaptive thinking and entrepreneurial drive but a lower level of excellence in execution."[14] In addition, they showed less evidence of interpersonal understanding and team facilitation than CEOs from Western countries but more focus on the greater good of the country. Compared to their counterparts in China and internationally, Indian CEOs spend a "disproportionate [sic] of their time coping with regulation and governance" issues.[15] In the paper and the longer book with the same title, the authors mention that they used behavioral event interviewing when they interviewed Indian CEOs for their research. It is important to realize that whenever this type of survey is done, the profile is based on the average for a range of personalities and organizations.

So, if the profile of the CEO in India is different from CEOs in some other parts of the world, how does that change competency-based interviews? Knowing that Indian CEOs have more focus on the *greater good of the country*, it is reasonable to assume that they want their management team to share that same value or competency. From a coaching perspective, I would encourage managers interested in working for well-regarded Indian companies like Tata Motors, Infosys, or Reliance Industries, to be prepared for interview questions about what they have done to make their community or country better. This same advice applies to senior managers interviewing with the Indian country head of a non-Indian company, because they need to *fit in* to the business community in India.

One of the major competencies that Indian CEOs rank lower in than their international counterparts is **Interpersonal Understanding**. This is particularly interesting because of the emphasis in India on IQ and the competition to get into their best universities, like IIT (Indian Institute of Technology). From an interview coaching perspective, the question is, does the CEO of the company see the need to change their culture and build the level of the competency, **Interpersonal Understanding**, in the organization? The answer may depend on how much of the organization's business is domestic or international. If the customers or employees come from a different culture, there may be more of a need to build this competency…or hire new managers or employees who are strong in this area. Or it may be influenced, very simply, by how important the key leaders in the organization think this competency is. An example of an interpersonal understanding question? *Give me an example of a situation you've been in where the ability to tune in to a customer's reaction made a difference.*

Because the culture in India is generally recognized as being more formal than that of most Western countries, plan to dress just a little more conservatively than you might for a Western interview. Saris are often worn by Indian women for business. Be respectful in the interview, just as you would be in any interview. It's what you need to do to get the position.

While India and Canada provide some good examples to consider, when you are interviewing in other places throughout the world, expect some differences. While many of the major competencies may stay the same, differences in culture and language can influence the way interviewers perceive your responses to competency-based interview questions. When you are interviewing for a position in a different culture than your own, do your homework. Remember, with the internet and new technology, the world is getting more interconnected, or flatter if you read Thomas L. Friedman's 2007 book, *The World is Flat*.

It is important to realize that competency-based interviews are being used throughout the world. One indicator? According to WorldCat, which tracks which libraries have specific books, in addition to libraries in the U.S., Canada, Australia, South Africa, and New Zealand, the first edition of *Competency-Based Interviews* is held by the libraries from the China European Business School, the Institute of Information Sciences in Slovenia, the American University in Cairo, and the Academic College of Tel Aviv. To quote J.R.R. Tolkien, the author of *The Lord of The Rings*, "The wide world is all about you; you can fence yourselves in, but you cannot forever fence it out." So get outside the fence, travel, live abroad, and realize you can learn from people from different countries and cultures. Even about competencies.

Key Points for Chapter 15

Get outside the fence, travel, live abroad, and realize you can learn from people from different countries and cultures. Even about competencies.

Key Questions	Answers
What decisions do global organizations have to make about competencies?	• Do they use the same competencies worldwide or define competencies differently based on country or culture? • Do they want one set of competencies worldwide? • Are organization leaders expected to demonstrate the same key leadership competencies wherever they work…while competencies for employees may be treated differently? • Do they choose to use the same competencies but adjust their behavioral indicators for different countries or cultures?

Key Questions	Answers
What needs to be considered when translating competencies from one language to another?	There are some subtleties, such as word connotation, that need to be considered.
How can you find examples of global competencies?	Google the name of an organization and words like *competencies* or *global competencies*.
What is the definition of intercultural competency?	The ability to function effectively in another culture.
Do we have intercultural competencies within the same country?	Yes, if our country has a diverse population.
What are the three major intercultural competencies identified by the Kozai Group?	Perception management, relationship management, and self-management.
What are the intercultural competencies identified by the Kozai Group?	**Perception Management:** Nonjudgmentalness, Inquisitiveness, Tolerance of Ambiguity, Cosmopolitanism, Category Inclusiveness **Relationship Management:** Relationship Interest, Interpersonal Engagement, Emotional Sensitivity, Social Flexibility, Self-Awareness **Self-Management:** Optimism, Self-Confidence, Self-Identity, Emotional Resilience, Non-Stress Tendency, Stress Management, Interest Flexibility
What is the definition of cosmopolitanism?	A natural interest in and curiosity about different countries and cultures.
Can you improve your rating on every intercultural competency?	Maybe not. Leading edge researchers are recognizing that personality traits are extremely difficult to change. So organizations may be better off hiring people who have characteristics, like social flexibility, that they need in certain positions.

Key Questions	Answers
What has caused so much emphasis on competencies in Canada?	It's the law in Canada. The Public Service Employment Act, which has been law since 1967, emphasizes merit, non-partisanship, fairness, access, transparency and representativeness. People hired into federal government jobs must have specific competencies, skills, and experience.
Why do they emphasize transparency in Canada?	It's the law. When you look at the material available online to Canadian government employees and candidates about behavioral event interviews, it is clear that their system is set up to be as transparent as possible.
How has The Canada Revenue Agency set up their interview process to reduce the chance a candidate will exaggerate or lie about an accomplishment in the interview?	Candidates are told not to lie, and they are asked to sign an agreement giving the agency the right to validate examples candidates use in the interview. Candidates need to provide interviewers a list of people who can confirm their examples. The agency has identified indicators of embellishment. When too many indicators of embellishment are used, it triggers a validation check.
Why is India considered so important?	It is the second most populous country and is expected to have the largest population by 2025. It has one of the fastest growing economies in the world.
What are some key differences between Indian CEOs and their counterparts in other countries/ cultures?	Indian CEOs: ◆ Demonstrate higher levels of adaptive thinking and entrepreneurial drive but lower levels of excellence in execution; ◆ Show less evidence of interpersonal understanding and team facilitation than CEOs from Western countries; ◆ Focus more on the "greater good of the country." ◆ Spend a "disproportionate of their time coping with regulation and governance" issues.
What should managers and professionals consider doing to prepare for interviews with major Indian companies?	Because of the focus on the *greater good of the country*, be prepared for interview questions about what you have done to make your community/ country better. Everything else you would plan to do to prepare for interviews elsewhere.

S. Laib
UM...I DON'T THINK "COMPETENT-SATIONAL" IS AN ACTUAL WORD...
RESUME
GEORGE W. BUSH

Chapter 13

Send a Thank-You Note, Follow Up, Get the Offer, and Negotiate

Imagine that you've just finished your final gymnastics routine at the Olympics. You've practiced for years and have spent a significant portion of your life on the uneven parallel bars and in floor exercises. You know you have worked hard with your coach, and you just gave a very good performance. Now you are waiting for your final score from the judges. Will you get the gold, the silver, or the bronze medal? Like a gymnast, you were just put through your paces during an interview and gave the performance of your life. You liked the interviewers you met. This is your own version of the Olympics because you know you really want this position.

The interviewers asked almost all of the competency-based interview questions you expected. Because you worked through the competencies and did a good job of anticipating questions, you were able to give thoughtful answers to prove how strong you are in each key competency area. You know that you did well in the interview—now you are waiting to find out whether you will get the offer. You're probably ready to relax for a bit, but it's still just a little too early for that. Don't celebrate just yet—you aren't finished with the process, because you haven't heard from the employer. What's left? First, you need to try to be as objective as possible and assess how the interview went. Ask yourself these questions:

- What did I do well?
- What could I have done during the interview to be perceived as a stronger candidate?

I believe that debriefing after the interview is extremely important. Talk to your career or interview coach, go through the questions and answers, and look for opportunities to fine-tune your answers to make them more specific, concise, logical, or positive. Ask yourself if there is anything you did, verbally or nonverbally, that may have sent a negative message to the interviewers. You may be good, but you can always be better. I tell students in communications classes that I'd probably give Dr. Martin Luther King, Jr. a 98 or 99 on his "I Have a Dream" speech, which is generally considered one of the best speeches of the 20th century. Your interviewing skills, like your writing and presentation skills, can always be brought to the next level. So what else is important at this point? You need to send a well-written, competency-based thank-you note to each interviewer, and then plan to follow up at the right time. When you get an offer you may decide to negotiate with the employer. If you don't get an offer you may choose to follow up to demonstrate your interest in being considered for other opportunities in the future.

Send a Thank-You Note

Hopefully you remembered to ask for business cards from each interviewer you met. If they didn't have business cards with them, you made sure to include their names in your notes, which you took immediately after the interview. You also jotted down some of the specific details that you remembered from each interview to enable you to write personal, nongeneric thank-you notes. And of course you made a list of the questions you were asked. Thank-you notes are still important in today's business world. They can make a positive difference in the interviewer's perception of you as a candidate. But they can also have a negative impact. I've seen candidates eliminated because they sent thank-you notes with poor grammar and smiley faces, or with the name of the interviewer or organization spelled incorrectly. Your thank-you notes should be as polished and professional as you are. So proofread each note and put it through spell-check. Use capital letters appropriately, use complete sentences, and always use good punctuation, grammar, and spelling. Avoid using smiley faces, Internet shorthand ("lol," "cul8r"), and emoticons.

In today's business environment, most candidates should to plan send their thank-you notes within 24 hours via e-mail. Think about how you want to be perceived—using e-mail shows that you are current with technology. The only exception to this recommendation that I can think of is with nonprofit organizations, where many professionals are still expected to write personal handwritten notes to donors and volunteers. According to Delphia York Duckens, Director, External Affairs for the Smithsonian National Museum of African American History and Culture, even nonprofits are beginning to change. She told me, "We're starting to see e-mail used more for thank-you notes and other communication." So if you are trying to make a decision about whether to send your thank-you note to a nonprofit using e-mail or snail mail, consider how technologically advanced the nonprofit is. As well, send the thank-you note between the hours of 6 a.m. and midnight, because your e-mail will show when it was sent, and you don't want to be perceived as an eccentric night owl. Even if you are! And finally, wait at least three hours after the interview to send your thank-you notes so that you don't appear desperate.

Steps to Writing a Well-Crafted, Competency-Based Thank-You Note

Before you start writing the thank-you note, ask yourself these questions:

- What competencies are needed for the position I interviewed for?
- Was there a competency the interviewers mentioned that I didn't talk about in the interview? Or one that I didn't give enough details about to prove that I am competent?
- Was I impressed with anything any of the interviewers discussed?
- Was there something I left out that was important or that I could have explained better?
- What did I learn about the organization, the corporate culture, and the management style that will help me explain more effectively why I am a good match for the position?

When you write the thank-you note:

- Address each thank-you note to a specific person, even if you were interviewed by group or panel. Individual, tailored thank-you notes are always more appreciated.
- First, tell the interviewer thank you—that you appreciate her time or the opportunity to have an interview. Tell her that you enjoyed meeting him and learning more about the position.
- Second, tell her something about how you are even more interested in the position and even more convinced that you would be successful in the position, now that you've spoken with her. Identify how your competencies match her needs (use competency synonyms to be a little more subtle but still get your point across) and will benefit her department or organization. Relate your comments to something that was said in the interview—for example, "I was particularly impressed when you talked to me about...."

- Third, tell her you are looking forward to hearing from her in the near future and would be happy to answer any questions or provide any additional information that she might need.
- Make sure you remember to put the interviewer's name at the top of the e-mail and your name at the bottom. If you want to start the e-mail with the words *Dear [interviewer's name]*, close with a salutation (*Sincerely* works best) before your name.

Always do a final edit with Spell Check to make sure the e-mail reflects your professionalism and attention to detail.

Follow Up

At the end of the interview most good interviewers will tell you:

★ What the next steps are.

★ How much time they'll need before getting back to you.

If they didn't give you this information, you should have directly asked for it by saying, "I'm very interested in this opportunity. What's the next step?" Also ask them, "When is a good time for me to follow up with you?" Many interviewers and human resources professionals are too optimistic about the timing and will, with good intentions, tell you they'll get back to you within a certain period of time, such as one or two weeks. Priorities in any organization are continually changing, and there are usually valid business reasons if the process takes longer than expected. During my years as a human resources professional, I learned to overestimate the time we'd need to give the candidate an answer to keep from disappointing him or her. Remember that interviewers always have other important projects, assignments, and even a crisis or two to deal with. Manage your own expectations and give them the benefit of the doubt.

Learn to double the amount of time the interviewer tells you it will take to get back to you after the interview. Be pleasantly surprised if he is able to respond to you sooner.

If an interviewer tells you to follow up in two or three weeks, do it. Don't be a pest, but be persistent and professional. Use your best judgment, but please be respectful of the interviewer's time. Don't even think about calling daily unless you are interviewing for a position as a stalker.

In most situations, following up every week or two is appropriate. If you are told the position has been put on hold, ask the interviewer when you should follow up to touch base with him.

Finally, if you receive an offer, call or e-mail the interviewers at other organizations you've interviewed with. Tell them that you've received an offer. If you are interested in their opportunity, let them know that you are still interested and it is your first choice (or one of your top choices).

Negotiate

Congratulations! You've just received a job offer, and even though you are excited, you know it could be better. What should you do now?

- ⋆ Thank the interviewer or human resources professional, and let him know that you really appreciate the offer.
- ⋆ Ask for the offer in writing. Let the employer decide how to send it to you. In most cases today, they will probably e-mail the offer and explain how to look up information about benefits on the organization's Website.
- ⋆ Tell the interviewer that you want to review all the information and that you are sure you are going to have some questions. Ask if it would work for him if you called him in two or three days with your answer (or questions).
- ⋆ Talk to your network to help you do some intelligence work. The president of the United States may have the CIA, but most of us can find out all sorts of information from the people we know—or the people they know—that could help us negotiate more effectively. Remember the theory behind six degrees of separation—namely, that we can get to anyone we want if we ask our contact's contact's contact's contact's contact's contact.
- ⋆ Try to find out information about the salary range for this position in your geographic area, whether the organization will negotiate, what's normal for vacation, and what special deals (signing bonuses, car allowances, bonuses, benefits, memberships, and so forth) the organization may have offered other people in similar jobs or at a similar level.
- ⋆ Do your homework and know what is likely to be negotiable and what is not. Salary and vacation are certainly negotiable in many organizations, particularly once you've had a few years

of work experience. Qualified benefit plans, including 401(k)s or other retirement plans, are set up organization-wide and are heavily regulated. Don't waste your bargaining chip trying to get an organization to make an exception for you on a plan that has legal restrictions. If you are working with a recruiter, he or she may know some of this information or be willing to help you find it.

- ★ Realize that negotiating well requires good information and good judgment. Each situation is different, and it is difficult to identify a set of rules that work in all situations. You probably would benefit by talking about the offer to someone with inside information or a good knowledge of the market in your field.
- ★ If you decide to negotiate, remember that your goal is win-win. You want the people you'll be working with to *want* to work with you after you've finished negotiating and accepted the position. Identify your top three to five priorities that you want to negotiate, and go through them during your first conversation. It is not fair to settle things one at a time and then come back to negotiate the next priority. You may get what you want in the short-term but lose the long-term trust you need to build effective working relationships and do the job. So treat the person representing the organization in the negotiation, whether your future manager or human resources professional, with respect.
- ★ Always emphasize the positives at the beginning of any negotiation, and let the other person know how excited you are about the opportunity. Tell the person representing the organization how impressed you are with the people there, and list everything good about the opportunity that you can think of. Then, explain again why you are such a good match or fit for the position. After that, say something such as, "I have to admit I was a little disappointed with the [salary, vacation, etc.], and I'm wondering if there's room to negotiate." Then pause and see what the person says.
- ★ Remember the old saying, "If you don't ask, you won't receive." You'll rarely have regrets if you negotiate with respect and professionalism, and you just may get what you want—and feel even better about accepting the job opportunity.

By the way, the judges just came back. Don't tell anyone, but you *did* win the gold.

Key Points for Chapter 13

Don't be a pest, but be persistent and professional.
If you don't ask, you won't receive.

Key Questions	Answers
Can you relax when the interview is over?	Not yet. You need to debrief, send a competency-based thank-you note, and follow up at the appropriate times.
What questions should you ask yourself after the interview?	What did I do well during the interview? What could I have done to be perceived as a stronger candidate by the interviewer?
What information do you need before writing your thank-you notes?	Make sure you have the correct name, title, and e-mail address for each interviewer. Look over your notes to come up with specific items that your interviewer mentioned to include in a personalized, tailored thank-you note.
How should you send your thank-you notes?	Use e-mail unless you have a very good reason to use snail mail. Send thank-you notes by e-mail within 24 hours after you leave the interview, but not within the first three hours. Avoid sending e-mails between midnight and 6 a.m.
What else should you remember about thank-you notes?	◆ Don't be overly informal. Capitalize where appropriate, check spelling/punctuation/grammar, and avoid Internet shorthand and emoticons. ◆ Write individualized notes to each interviewer. ◆ Edit the note and put it through Spell Check.
How do you write a competency-based thank-you note?	Reiterate how your experience addresses the competencies the employer needs to be successful. Back up your point about the relevant experience by giving a specific example.
When should you follow up after the interview?	It depends. Hopefully the interviewer told you when you can expect to hear back from him. Double whatever timeframe he gave you. If the interviewer told you when to follow up, call when you were told to call.

Key Questions	Answers
What should you do immediately after you receive an offer?	◆ Thank the person giving you the offer. ◆ Ask for the offer in writing. ◆ Tell the interviewer you're sure you are going to have some questions, and you'll get back to her once you've reviewed the offer and benefits.
How do you prepare for negotiating with a potential employer?	◆ Do some intelligence work—learn about typical salaries for the position in your geographic area, whether the organization has a history of negotiating, what's normal for vacation, and other benefits and perks. ◆ Know what is usually negotiable (salary and vacations, for example) and what is never negotiable (401(k) and other retirement vehicles). ◆ Decide what is the most important item, and then add two to three other things to focus on during your negotiation with the employer.
What outcome do you want when you negotiate your offer?	Win-win. You want to get the most you can while ensuring the key people at the organization will still want to work with you.
Why should you try to negotiate with the employer?	Many employers will offer you only the basics because they expect you to negotiate. If you don't ask for the extra vacation, salary, signing bonus, or better relocation package, you won't get it. If you don't try, you may regret it. If you do negotiate, you may just be surprised at what you are able to get.

Chapter 14

Actively Manage Your Career in Competency-Based Organizations

Look at a day when you are supremely satisfied at the end. It's not a day when you lounge around doing nothing; it's when you've had everything to do, and you've done it.

—Margaret Thatcher

Congratulations! You've learned what it takes to win in a competency-based interview, and now you're getting ready to start that great job you really wanted. You're excited about the opportunity and you want to do well. What do you need to know to actively manage your career in a competency-based organization? How can you capitalize on your promotion to a new position in a different part of your own organization? When you were in school you learned that the best students always made an effort to understand their assignments and do what the teachers asked. In his book *All I Really Need to Know I Learned in Kindergarten*, Robert Fulghum makes the case that we probably learned this type of behavior when we were very young. In your new position you need to become a good student again. It is important to understand the system and learn how to work within it if you want to be successful.

You've already taken the first few steps toward managing your career in a competency-based organization. You've identified the competencies you need to be successful in the position, and you've thought about how your accomplishments help prove you are competent in the most critical areas. In addition, you've learned how to talk about your accomplishments when answering competency-based behavioral questions. As you continue your career you need to be aware of how important it is to build, track, and master the right competencies. To help ensure that you are perceived as the star that I know you are, I have seven suggestions for what you can do to actively manage your career the competency-based way:

1. Learn to write competency-based accomplishment statements to use in employee development plans, performance appraisals, and other situations.
2. Set up and use a system to track your competencies.
3. Develop your critical competencies to a higher level.
4. Identify and overcome any competency gaps.
5. Develop competencies you'll need for future positions.
6. Promote your career by making sure your managers know your competencies.
7. Give your manager a current list of your accomplishments in each key competency area before your performance appraisal.

Let's look at each of these recommendations in more detail.

Learn to Write Competency-Based Accomplishment Statements to Use in Employee Development Plans, Performance Appraisals, and Other Situations.

Think about your answers to competency-based interview questions. As you prepared for the interview you put together a list of your accomplishments in each relevant competency area. You've already thought about your examples. Now you just have to turn them into true accomplishment statements—in other words, write them down! Here are a few other tips about how to write effective competency-based accomplishment statements:

- Focus on your accomplishments proving your competencies.
- Say as much as you can in as few words as you can. Don't use complete sentences or extraneous words that don't add to the content. Be concise.
- Always start with an action word.
- Think through the situation/task/problem, action, and result—of every accomplishment. Decide whether the result, the action, or the process is going to matter the most to the employer, and then make that the first part of your accomplishment statement.
- Try to give numbers, statistics, or financial figures to help the reader understand the scope of the assignment or project. Be specific, and give enough details to be credible.

- ★ Assume that your readers are intelligent but may not know the details about your immediate business or professional area.
- ★ Make your accomplishment statements as strong as you can without lying. Remember to frame your answer in the most positive way possible while still being honest.
- ★ Whenever possible try to include high-profile examples that your senior executives will know about.

Learning to write targeted competency-based accomplishment statements is one of the most important steps to managing your career effectively in competency-based organizations—actually, in almost any type of organization. For more tips on how to use these statements to advocate for yourself or your team through performance reviews, you might want to read my third book, *Competency-Based Performance Reviews.*

Two examples of effective competency-based accomplishment statements:

- Worked as key member of focus group looking at best practices for data management; helped create business case for buying more disk space.
- Recognized by vice president for successfully leading project team reducing utility processing from three hours to 10 minutes per day and increasing accuracy by 30 percent; improved customer relationships with six major clients.

Set Up and Use a System to Track Your Competencies

It is important to spend some time setting up a system to track your accomplishments and the competencies that are demonstrated in each accomplishment. Very few, if any, organizations have developed this kind of system for their employees, so you probably need to think about setting up a system that will work for you. Whether you use a Word table, an Excel spreadsheet, an Access database, software programs for your phone, or an old-fashioned paper filing system, you should include accomplishments related to:

- ★ The competencies identified for your current position.
- ★ The competencies you would need for positions for which you would like to be considered in the future.

Develop Your Critical Competencies to a Higher Level

Once you know the critical competencies for your current position, you need to identify the accomplishments that prove your own competence in each area. Look for opportunities to gain experience showing that your work is at an even higher, more sophisticated level of competency. Ask to be considered for certain assignments. Find a mentor or a coach to help you develop. Take classes offered by your organization or at colleges and universities or in the community. Consider doing volunteer work or teaching classes at a university or college to build your competencies.

Identify and Overcome Any Competency Gaps

In some cases, your weakest competency areas can offer you the biggest opportunities for growth. What are the competencies that you cannot prove because you do not have any direct experience in those areas to draw from? These are your competency gaps, and they should be bridged and eliminated. In many cases, people decide that they can compensate for their gaps by using other competencies. Perception matters. The key question in this case is whether your manager perceives the gap as a weakness that needs to be overcome. If she does, work on it!

When a good employee transfers to another functional area or department, it is reasonable to expect some competency gaps. Think about an engineer transferring into finance or sales, or a human resources manager who becomes a line manager in manufacturing. In these cases, the new manager and other key people typically put together an extensive on-the-job and classroom training schedule, and actively coach the transferred employee. Everyone benefits when the transfer is recognized as successful and the transferred employee has overcome his or her competency gaps.

Develop Competencies You'll Need for Future Positions

Where do you want to be in five or 10 years? In addition to the competencies you need for your current position, you need to start doing some work now, on the front end, that will help you prove you have the competencies you need for the higher level opportunities that come later. If you do this when you are being considered for your next promotion, it should be clear to the critical decision-makers that you have been working at that higher level for some time. You've already proved your competence in the key areas required to do a good job.

Promote Your Career by Making Sure Your Managers Know Your Competencies

Have you ever complained that you didn't get an assignment or position because the manager making the decision didn't realize that you had experience in a certain area? Don't let that happen to you again. Make sure your managers know about any competencies and accomplishments of yours that are *not* being used in your current position but that could be used in the future. For example, if you know your company is looking at an acquisition in Argentina and you lived there for three years before college, make sure the right managers know that you have the competencies of **Interpersonal Understanding** and **Multicultural Sensitivity** and, perhaps more important, that you can *prove* them. Even if you mentioned this to your manager two years ago in your interview, remind her that you are bicultural and bilingual and would love to have the opportunity to work on the acquisition.

When you have an accomplishment related to one of the critical competencies for your position, make sure your manager knows. Simply call your manager over to your office to tell her how excited you are because a particular project is going well, and describe the results. If you are working virtual, include the news about your accomplishment in a telephone session with your manager.

Give Your manager a Current List of Your Accomplishments in Each Key Competency Area Before Your Performance Appraisal

Because you will be tracking your accomplishments by competency area for several months or even a full year, you should be ready to provide this information to your manager whenever it could be of help to him. In terms of helping your own career, however, one of the best times to communicate this information to your manager is three or four weeks before your performance appraisal. List each accomplishment under the most relevant competency. You may also wish to identify the other competencies shown by the accomplishment for your manager.

Conclusion

If you consider competencies when you actively manage your career, and you follow the tips in this chapter, you will be ahead of most of the people that you currently consider your competition in the organization. I'm not surprised—I always knew you were a star!

Key Points for Chapter 14

"Look at a day when you are supremely satisfied at the end. It's not a day when you lounge around doing nothing; it's when you've had everything to do, and you've done it." —Margaret Thatcher

Key Questions	Answers
What can you do to manage your career the competency-based way?	◆ Learn to write competency-based accomplishment statements to use in employee development plans, self-appraisals, and other situations. ◆ Set up and use a system to track your competencies. ◆ Develop your critical competencies to a higher level. ◆ Identify and overcome any competency gaps. ◆ Develop competencies you'll need for future positions. ◆ Promote your career to your managers. ◆ Give your manager a list of your accomplishments in each competency area immediately before your performance appraisals.
What should you keep in mind when you write competensy-based accomplishment statements?	Build on the accomplishments you've identified to answer competency-based interview questions: ◆ Focus on your accomplishments proving competencies. ◆ Say as much as you can in as few words as you can. ◆ Don't use complete sentences or extraneous "filler" words. ◆ Always start with an action word. ◆ Make sure you've thought about the SAR of every accomplishment. ◆ Decide whether the result, the action, or the process is going to matter the most to the employer, and make that the first part of your accomplishment statement. ◆ Try to give numbers, statistics, or financial figures to help the reader understand the project/assignment scope. Be specific, and give enoughdetails to be credible. ◆ Assume that readers are intelligent but may not know the details about your business or professional area. ◆ Make your statements as positive as you can without lying. ◆ Include high-profile examples that your senior executives might know about, if possible.

Key Questions	Answers
What type of system should you set up to track your competencies?	If your employer doesn't have a system, figure out what will work the best for you. You can use a Word table, Excel spreadsheet, database, or old-fashioned filing system.
What do you need to track?	Accomplishments and the competencies they show.
What do you need to remember when you have input into your training and development or future assignments?	Use these opportunities to develop your competencies to a higher level for your current position *and* future job possibilities. You can also use this as a way to overcome any competency gaps you might have.
What else can you do to help manage your career in a competency-based organization?	◆ Make every effort to communicate with your managers about your accomplishments in key competency areas. ◆ Don't be overly modest. ◆ Use the language of competencies. ◆ Give your manager a list of your accomplishments sorted by competency area three to four weeks before your performance appraisal.

S. Laito
HOW DID THE MOVIE "KINDERGARTEN COP" PREPARE YOU FOR A CAREER IN POLITICS?...
RESUME
ARNOLD SCHWARZENEGGER

Chapter 15

Use Competency-Based Resumes to Get Your Next Interview

Man's mind, once stretched by a new idea, never regains its original dimensions.
—Oliver Wendell Holmes

When I first read the above quote, I thought about my new idea of competency-based resumes. It's true that my mind has never been the same, and I'd really like to think it is better. So with all due respect to Mr. Holmes, please substitute the words *a person's mind* for *man's mind.* Giving employees some background on competencies and how they can handle competency-based interviews and learn to thrive in a competency-based organization is another new idea. You've spent most of this book learning how to be successful in a competency-based interview to help you get the job you really want. In the previous chapter, you learned how to write competency-based accomplishment statements to help you advocate for yourself. You also started thinking about how to track and develop your competencies and how to communicate more effectively with your managers about your competencies. You're in that great job now, you're doing well, and you've proven how competent you are over an extended period of time. But don't get too comfortable. It's time to stretch yourself by starting to think about your next opportunity, and you need to be ready. It's time to write your first competency-based resume or revise the competency-based resume you used to win your last position.

Why You Should Write a Competency-Based Resume

Competency-based resumes are much more effective than more traditional resumes. They give you an edge with employers because they target the competencies that employers are looking for in today's labor market. Competency-based resumes consider the employer's needs first, and then help prove that you match what the employer is looking for. A well-written, competency-based resume includes crisp, targeted accomplishment statements and a summary section aimed at the competencies the employer needs to be successful now and in the future. Why should you use a competency-based resume? It will sell your experience more effectively to employers and increase your chance of getting the interview. Even in non-competency-based organizations, a competency-based resume will give you an edge because it is written to target the real needs of the employer.

Steps to Writing a Competency-Based Resume

The approach to writing competency-based resumes is different from the way you may have written your resume in the past. To write an effective, well-crafted competency-based resume, you need to follow these steps:

1. Identify competencies for the position.
2. Think about what you have done that demonstrates expertise or experience in each of these competencies.
3. Develop accomplishment statements for as many of the competencies as you can.
4. Write the summary section that emphasizes your experience and strengths related to the key competencies for the position.
5. Determine which competency-based resume format—chronological, functional, direct competency, or combination—best fits your needs, and prepare your first draft of the resume.
6. Remember to include sections on your education and any other information relevant to potential employers.
7. Add additional competency-related accomplishment statements and, if you still have space, other accomplishment statements.
8. Prioritize competency-related phrases in your summary section and competency-based accomplishments within the appropriate sections of the resume.
9. Review and polish your resume. Ask other professionals for input.
10. Finalize your resume. Develop an electronic version of the resume with a keyword summary section.

Writing an effective competency-based resume should feel natural to you. You've already gone through the process of identifying competencies for your last position. Now you need to repeat the process and identify the competencies for the new position you are interested in. You've also learned how to write effective competency-based accomplishment statements, and have kept track of your accomplishments in a table, spreadsheet, database, or filing system. Refer back to Chapter 14 if you need to review these career management tips, and pull out your list of accomplishments before you beginn to write your resume.

Example of a Competency-Based Resume

Let's look at one example of a competency-based resume. This particular resume is a competency-based functional resume for the same financial sales professional whose answers to competency-based interview questions are included in Chapter 10. We chose to use this format because we wanted to emphasize her accomplishments in certain key categories that were important to the organization she was interested in working for.

Please know that what makes a resume competency-based is the content, not the format. Each accomplishment statement is competency-based. The summary also addresses the competencies.

There's more than one possible format for a competency-based resume. You can choose to write a competency-based chronological resume that looks more traditional and then focus on your work history with accomplishments listed under each job. Direct competency resumes list your accomplishments by competency and are good to use when you want to provide your manager with a list of your accomplishments before your performance appraisal. Of course you need to stay current and realize that resume styles change through time. Using the competency-based approach to writing resumes only makes more sense as I'm reviewing this material for this new edition of the book.

Donna Johnson's resume shown on pages 182–183 is a good example of a well-crafted competency-based resume. (Please know that I helped my client write this resume, but a few changes have been made to protect her privacy. I've changed her name, contact information, and the name of an employer or two.)

Once Donna identified the position she was interested in, we were able to determine the key competencies and write targeted competency-based accomplishment statements. Then we worked on the summary section.

Donna B. Johnson

3202 Jasmine
Denver, CO 80205

303 899-6508
johnson2@sbcglobal.net

Summary

Finance professional with strong interest in financial analysis and sales. Proven track record of developing financial models to streamline processes. Recognized for consistent ranking as top producer, understanding complex financial information and communicating financial data to clients to encourage investment. Strengths include results orientation, analytical and teaching/ training skills, resourcefulness, and initiative.

Licenses: Series 7, 63, 65 and 24 and Group 1.

Accomplishments

Financial Analysis

- Recognized for developing first proprietary sell-to-cover model at company to calculate number of stock options to sell at set market price; increased customer satisfaction 15% and created opportunity for additional commissions.
- Developed first Excel spreadsheet at company to calculate taxes for exercising stock options for United Kingdom residents; provided competitive advantage to obtain 100% of IBM stock option business in United Kingdom; provided additional $90,000 per year in gross commission.
- Audited online system for exercising stock options at firm; analyzed data and recommended changes to improve visual presentation and quality of customer directions; increased online order submission 5%.
- Prepared competitive analysis of financial statements for five major oil companies while working as summer intern at Amoco.

Financial Sales/Marketing

- Ranked in top four of 40 retirement specialists nationally at Fidelity for 12 consecutive months, 2001–2002.
- Identified opportunity to increase assets by allowing customers to maintain their investments positions; persuaded three senior managers to support change in business practice; increased retained assets by 20%.
- Increased long term care insurance sales by 10%; designed and delivered long term care sales seminar for 15 retail brokers.
- Produced $180,000 in first year commissions as Financial Advisor at American Express; consistently ranked in top 25% of peer group.
- Recognized by manager for increasing small loan revenues 25%; created solicitation campaign for loans between $500–$1,000.
- Developed risk management program to collect delinquent accounts; reduced 30 day delinquency 30%.

Donna B. Johnson
Page 2

Accomplishments (continued)
Financial Training/Planning

- Trained 15 financial consultants on how to educate clients about annuities, long term care insurance and health insurance; increased sales 30%.
- Delivered training program on mortgage disclosure documentation, loan documentation and loan processing using proprietary system to 40 new employees.
- Developed training for 27 financial advisors at American Express on presenting client seminars for retirement, planning, college planning, and estate planning.
- Created financial plans for 150 individuals and 30 small businesses as American Express Financial Advisor 1998-2000.

Work History
Bank of America, Denver, CO 2005–Present
Vice President, Market Investments
National Financial, Denver, CO 2002–2005
Stock Options Department Supervisor, 2003–2005
Financial Consultant, 2002-2003
Fidelity Investments, Denver, CO 2000–2002
Senior Retirement Specialist
American Express Financial Advisors, Dallas, TX 1998–2000
Financial Advisor
Beneficial Inc., Denver, CO 1994–1998
Branch Manager, 1996–1998
Assistant Branch Manager, 1995–1996
Branch Service Manager, 1994–1995

Education
Bachelor of Science, Marketing and International Business
University of Colorado, Boulder, CO

Summary or Profile

This section is one of the most important parts of any resume. When it is well written, it sells your background to the employer. It has replaced the objective on the resume because it is so much more effective at communicating the most important reasons the employer should consider you for the position.

One approach to writing a good summary section is to start with your professional title or the title listed for the position you are interested in. Then write about your expertise, your job-related strengths, and your strengths in the relevant competency areas. Some career experts prefer to create a bulleted list of your strengths; others don't. Please be aware that career coaches have different styles of writing summary sections. To ensure that your resume opens those doors for you, the summary should be competency-based.

Technical Skills

You should plan to have a technical skills section if your knowledge of software, hardware, or specific technical tools is required before a hiring manager will consider you for a position.

Education

Please make every effort to check this section of your resume for accuracy. Although I believe in putting the best possible spin you can on your background, you either have a college degree or you don't. Every year, it seems that we hear about a new example of someone who is in trouble for claiming a degree that he doesn't quite have. For example, in 2002, the athletic director for Dartmouth College resigned after his employer found out that he had not completed the master's degree he had listed on his resume. Please know that your educational credentials can be easily checked by the employer. As a general rule, if your degree is more than 10 years old, leave the graduation date off your resume.

Other Competency-Based Resume Tips

- ✭ Prioritize your accomplishments on the resume within each section to emphasize the experience and competencies that matter the most to the employer.
- ✭ Expect to use two pages on your resume unless you have less than 10 years of work experience, in which case you should have a one-page resume.

- ☆ Say as much as you can in as few words as you can.
- ☆ Always have a professional-looking e-mail address as part of your contact information. Consider setting up a new e-mail address just for your job search.
- ☆ Use your cell phone number on the resume. Don't waste space identifying a phone number as a phone number or an e-mail address as an e-mail address.
- ☆ If you include an "Other Information" or "Community Activities" section, only include information proving you'd be effective at a specific job. Don't include anything controversial such as religion or politics unless you are interested in a position with a church, mosque, or temple; with a political organization; or as an elected official.
- ☆ If you have some special issues, such as not working for an extended period of time, consider talking with a professional about the best way to handle your situation on the resume. You might want to use a more traditional chronological resume to help the reader focus more on your accomplishments than on your work history. If you have been in one position for more than five years, you might choose to write a combination-style resume, which would show your accomplishments in your most recent job broken into a few important categories or competencies. Each situation is different, and a savvy professional can help you figure out the best way to position your resume to show your competencies and strengths the most effectively.
- ☆ *Plan to rewrite or revise your resume for every new job opportunity.* Once you have developed your first competency-based resume, though, you should have most of the information you'll need to target future opportunities.
- ☆ Avoid using all capital letters in your resume unless you are writing about a country or organization identified by its initials, such as the UK, the CIA, or the IRS. This recommendation (new to the second edition) is based on the fact that ALL CAPS are often interpreted as yelling at the reader. So, don't yell on your resume!

If you want more help with writing competency-based resumes, read my book *Competency-Based Resumes: How to Bring Your Resume to the Top of the Pile* (Career Press, November 2004) for more examples and details about how to write extremely good resumes targeting the competencies the employers need. (If you liked this book, I'm confident that you'll also enjoy *Competency-Based Resumes*.)

Key Points for Chapter 15

"Focusing on the competencies the employer is looking for is a very powerful way to approach one's next job." —Ward Klein, CEO, Energizer

Key Questions	Answers
Why should you write a competency-based resume?	Competency-based resumes: ◆ Are more effective than traditional resumes. ◆ Are targeted to meet the employer's needs. ◆ Sell your experience that matters to the employer
What are the steps to writing a competency-based resume?	1. Identify competencies for the position. 2. Think about what you have done that demonstrates experience in each key competency. 3. Develop accomplishment statements for as many of the competencies as you can. 4. Write the summary section to emphasize your experience and strengths related to the key competencies for the position. 5. Determine which competency-based resume format—chronological, functional, direct competency, or combination—best fits your needs, and prepare your first draft with that in mind. 6. Remember to include sections on your education and any other information relevant to potential employers. 7. Add additional competency-related accomplishment statements and, if you still have space, other accomplishment statements. 8. Prioritize competency-related phrases in your summary section and competency-based accomplishments within appropriate sections. 9. Review and polish your resume. Ask other professionals for input. 10. Finalize your resume. Develop an electronic version of the resume with a key summary section.

Key Questions	Answers
What makes a resume competency-based?	The content, not the format.
What are the different formats you can use for your competency-based resume?	◆ Competency-based chronological. ◆ Competency-based functional. ◆ Direct competency. ◆ Combination.
What is important to remember about the Summary section of your resume?	◆ If it is well written, it will sell your background to the employer. ◆ Start with a professional title, then write your expertise, job-related strengths, and your strengths in the relevant competency areas.
When should you include a Technical Skills section in your resume?	If your knowledge of hardware, software, or technical tools is required before the employer will consider you for a position.
What is important to remember for the Education section of your resume?	◆ Don't claim a degree or educational credential you don't have. ◆ If your degree is more than 10 years old, don't include your graduation date.

Key Questions	Answers
What else should you know before writing a competency-based resume?	◆ Prioritize your accomplishments within each section to emphasize experience and competencies that matter the most to the employer. ◆ Expect to use two pages on your resume, unless you have less than 10 years of work experience. ◆ Say as much as you can in as few words as you can. ◆ Always use an e-mail address that sounds professional as part of your contact information. ◆ Use your cell phone number on the resume. ◆ Don't waste space identifying phone numbers or e-mail addresses as such; people know what they are. ◆ If you include an Other Information or Community Activities section, only include information that proves you will be effective at a specific job. As a general rule, don't include anything controversial such as religion or politics. ◆ If you have a special issue, such as a gap in your employment history, consider talking with a professional about the best way to handle this on your resume. ◆ Plan to rewrite or revise your resume for every new job opportunity. ◆ Don't use all caps—you don't want it to look as though you're yelling.
If you want to learn more about competency-based resumes, what should you do?	Read my book *Competency-Based Resumes: How to Bring Your Resume to the Top of the Pile* (Career Press, 2004).

Chapter 16

Think Long-Term and Make Change Work for You

The real voyage of discovery consists not in seeking new landscapes, but in having new eyes.

—Marcel Proust

When I first read Proust's quote, I thought about the changes competencies have brought to the landscape of interviewing, for people who want to work at the best, most sophisticated companies around the world. In this book you've learned some important ways to make competency-based systems work for you. As of this writing competencies have been in use in the business world for more than 30 years, but today's competency-based systems are much more sophisticated than they used to be. They are continuing to grow and evolve. You don't have to seek a new landscape—the landscape itself has changed. The landscape has changed everywhere, and your job is to make sure that you notice and keep up with these changes.

Because some employees and candidates resist change, they may never see that the system around them has changed. Many of us can remember secretaries who didn't think they had to learn about computers or word processing. Technology had changed the landscape of these jobs. If they didn't change their views and learn to work with computers, these employees became obsolete pretty quickly. Technology, everything from social networking to virtual assessment centers, has continued to change the way we do things, including competency-based interviewing.

If you don't recognize and adapt to change, you'll become obsolete.

What can we expect for the future? How will the landscape change? And how will our perception of those changes affect our success? In the short term, you can expect more and more organizations to continue to work with competencies. It just makes sense. If your company isn't working with competencies yet, there's a good chance it will in the future. Thinking about what is most important to your employer first will help you be more successful even in a non-competency-based organization.

Many of the most sophisticated employers have worked closely with consultants to develop effective competency-based human resources systems that are working well for them. Managers at these organizations usually make the decision to use competency-based systems because they see it as a way to help them improve the overall performance of their employees.

Organizations with effective competency-based systems in place are in a strong position to build the key characteristics that it will take to be even more successful in the future. Their managers recruit, interview, and hire employees who are strong in the competencies they need. They evaluate their employees based on goals and competencies, and coach or train their employees to develop the competencies the organization needs to ensure success.

The best organizations have invested considerable time and money into these competency-based systems. But are they working as well as they could? Based on my consulting, the answer is no. Employers need to collaborate with their employees to make their competency-based systems work more effectively. There are six major reasons it makes sense for employers to partner with employees and make more of an effort to explain their own competency-based system to their employees.[1]

1. **To improve the competency levels of their employees faster.** If each employee understands the competency-based system and takes responsibility for managing his or her relevant competencies (in addition to training or coaching provided by the organization), the overall competency levels within the organization will improve much faster.
2. **To provide managers with better information about the competencies of their employees.** If employees advocate for themselves more effectively by providing better-written, clearer competency-based information about their accomplishments in performance reviews and development plans, or if they are able to give more specific explanations during competency-based interviews, it will give managers the information they need to make better decisions about assignments and opportunities.

3. **To enable companies to sell their services more effectively to competency-based customers.** For companies providing consulting, engineering, project management, or architectural work to competency-based organizations, it just makes sense for the proposed project team to develop competency-based resumes to include in the proposal package targeting the competencies the decision-makers are measured against. When the competency-based customer asks to interview the project team, the interviewees will be more successful if they are prepared for competency-based interviews. (Of course, improving the way you present your employees cannot overcome an extremely high bid for the contract, but it *can* make a difference in other cases.)
4. **To empower employees and improve morale.** If employees understand what they can do to actively manage their careers in competency-based systems, they are much more likely to buy into the system and be committed to making it work.
5. **To support diversity efforts.** By making more of an effort to train employees about competencies in their organizations, employers are demystifying what it takes to get ahead. On a practical level, they are helping to clarify the rules for everyone, without regard to race, sex, age, national origin, or disability status. More employees have a chance to be successful, and a wider variety of employees will actually *be* successful.
6. **To improve the quality of employee development and succession planning.** If managers have better access to good information about the competencies of the candidates for promotions, they can do a better job with succession planning and assigning projects to help prepare candidates for more challenging roles. Learning to communicate more effectively about your competencies to managers simply helps the key decision-makers make better decisions about your future opportunities.

Because it makes business sense, expect to see the better employers offer their employees more training about what they can do to be successful in the company's competency-based system. When I've worked with managers at companies such as American Express and BP to offer this type of program, there's been a strong level of interest from the employees. They recognize that the system has changed, and they want to know what they can do to be more successful on the new playing field.

At BP, the human resources department in Houston sponsored a pilot program called "How to Thrive in BP's Competency-Based System." My contact in human resources sent an e-mail to 200 people inviting them to a lunch-and-learn session. Within an hour, 100 people had responded saying they were interested in attending. Likewise, at American Express, one of the IT directors sponsored an initial program teaching employees how to thrive in their own competency-based system. I trained them to be more aware of the relevant competencies and showed them examples of competency-based accomplishment statements. The next step focused on teaching the same group how to write effective competency-based accomplishment statements for their employee development plans and employee questionnaires before mid-year and year-end performance reviews. In addition to formally sponsored training programs, special interest groups within larger companies sometimes bring in guest speakers. The Women's Network within JPMorganChase sponsored me to come in and speak to its members about how to be more successful working within its competency-based system, and I've spoken to the Latino Business Resource Group at one of the major refineries.

When you see your own organization begin to offer these types of programs to give employees tools that they can use to thrive with competencies, be one of the first to take advantage of the opportunity. Learn everything you can about the competencies for your current position and possible future positions. Think about what competencies are important for success now and in the future. Of course, while you're doing that, remember to continue to do your job! Understanding how competencies can work for you and help you be more successful is critical to help you plan and navigate your career for the future. Being smart and using this information to help advocate for yourself within your organization can make a difference.

Finally, learning about competencies will help you see your professional future with new eyes, eyes that are no longer limited to only seeing opportunities in your own neighborhood, city, or country. There's an exciting world out there. Your eyes may still be brown or blue or green or hazel, but your vision will be sharper, and you will now increase your chances of realizing your career goals. Make competency-based interviews work for you!

Appendix A

List of Core Competencies

The list of competencies included in this appendix was identified by the authors, Edward J. Cripe and Richard S. Mansfield in their book *The Value-Added Employee* (Butterworth-Heinermann, 2002). The focus is on 31 major competencies, along with the behaviors associated with each.

I. Competencies Dealing with People

The Leading Others Cluster

- **Establishing Focus**: The ability to develop and communicate goals in support of the business mission.
  - Acts to align own unit's goals with the strategic direction of the business.
  - Ensures that people in the unit understand how their work relates to the business mission.
  - Ensures that everyone understands and identifies with the unit's mission.
  - Ensures that the unit develops goals and a plan to help fulfill the business mission.
- **Providing Motivational Support**: The ability to enhance others' commitment to their work.
  - Recognizes and rewards people for their achievements.
  - Acknowledges and thanks people for their contributions.
  - Expresses pride in the group and encourages people to feel good about their accomplishments.
  - Finds creative ways to make people's work rewarding.

- Signals own commitment to a process by being personally present and involved at key events.
- Identifies and promptly tackles morale problems.
- Gives talks or presentations that energize groups.

▶ **Fostering Teamwork**: As a team member, the ability and desire to work cooperatively with others on a team; as a team leader, the ability to demonstrate interest, skill, and success in getting groups to learn to work together.

Behavior for Team Members

- Listens and responds constructively to other team members ideas.
- Offers support for others' ideas and proposals.
- Is open with other team members about his/her concerns.
- Expresses disagreement constructively
- Reinforces team members for their contributions.
- Gives honest and constructive feedback to other team members.
- Provides assistance to others when they need it.
- Works for solutions that all team members can support.
- Shares his/her expertise with others.
- Seeks opportunities to work on teams as a means to develop experience and knowledge.
- Provides assistance, information, or support to others, to build or maintain relationships with them.

Behavior for Team Leaders

- Provides opportunities for people to learn to work together as a team.
- Enlists the active participation of everyone.
- Promotes cooperation with other work units.
- Ensures that all team members are treated fairly.
- Recognizes and encourages the behaviors that contribute to teamwork.

▶ **Empowering Others**: The ability to convey confidence in employees ability to be successful, especially at challenging new tasks; delegating significant responsibility and authority; allowing employees freedom to decide how they will accomplish their goals and resolve issues.

- Gives people latitude to make decisions in their own sphere of work.

- Is able to let others make decisions and take charge.
- Encourages individuals and groups to set their own goals, consistent with business goals.
- Expresses confidence in the ability of others to be successful.
- Encourages groups to resolve problems on their own; avoids prescribing a solution.

▸ **Managing Change**: The ability to demonstrate support for innovation and for organizational changes needed to improve the organization's effectiveness; initiating, sponsoring, and implementing organizational change; helping others to successfully manage organizational change.

Employee Behaviors

- Personally develops a new method or approach.
- Proposes new approaches, methods, or technologies.
- Develops better, faster, or less expensive ways to do things.

Manager/Leader Behaviors

- Works cooperatively with others to produce innovative solutions.
- Takes the lead in setting new business directions, partnerships, policies, or procedures.
- Seizes opportunities to influence the future direction of an organizational unit or the overall business.
- Helps employees to develop a clear understanding of what they will need to do differently, as a result of changes in the organization.
- Implements or supports various management activities.
- Establishes structures and processes to plan and manage the orderly implementation of change.
- Helps individuals and groups manage the anxiety associated with significant change.
- Facilitates groups or teams through the problem-solving and creative-thinking processes leading to the development and implementation of new approaches, systems, structures, and methods.

▸ **Developing Others**: The ability to delegate responsibility and to work with others and coach them to develop their capabilities.

- Provides helpful, behaviorally specific feedback to others.
- Shares information, advice, and suggestions to help others be more successful; provides effective coaching.

- Gives people assignments that will help develop their abilities.
- Regularly meets with employees to review their developmental progress.
- Recognizes and reinforces people's developmental efforts and improvements.
- Expresses confidence in others ability to be successful.

- **Managing Performance**: The ability to take responsibility for one's own or one's employees' performance, by setting clear goals and expectations, tracking progress against the goals, ensuring feedback, and addressing performance problems and issues promptly.

Behaviors for employees

- With his manager, sets specific, measurable goals that are realistic but challenging, with dates for accomplishment.
- With his manager, clarifies expectations about what will be done and how.
- Enlists his managers support in obtaining the information, resources, and training needed to accomplish his work effectively.
- Promptly notifies his manager about any problems that affect his ability to accomplish planned goals.
- Seeks performance feedback from his manager and from others with whom he interacts on the job.
- Prepares a personal development plan with specific goals and a timeline for their accomplishment.
- Takes significant action to develop skills needed for effectiveness in current or future job.

Behaviors for managers

- Ensures that employees have clear goals and responsibilities.
- Works with employees to set and communicate performance standards that are specific and measurable.
- Supports employees in their efforts to achieve job goals.
- Stays informed about employees' progress and performance through both formal methods and informal methods.
- Provides specific performance feedback, both positive and corrective, as soon as possible after an event.
- Deals firmly and promptly with performance problems; lets people know what is expected of them and when.

The Communication and Influencing Cluster

- **Attention to Communication**: The ability to ensure that information is passed on to others who should be kept informed.
  - Ensures that others involved in a project or effort are kept informed about developments and plans.
  - Ensures that important information from his management is shared with his employees and others as appropriate.
  - Shares ideas and information with others who might find them useful.
  - Uses multiple channels or means to communicate important messages.
  - Keeps his manager informed about progress and problems; avoids surprises.
  - Ensures that regular, consistent communication takes place.
- **Oral Communication**: The ability to express one's self clearly in conversations and interactions with others.
  - Speaks clearly and can be easily understood.
  - Tailors the content of speech to the level and experience of the audience.
  - Uses appropriate grammar and choice of words in oral speech.
  - Organizes ideas clearly in oral speech.
  - Expresses ideas concisely in oral speech.
  - Maintains eye contact when speaking with others.
  - Summarizes or paraphrases his understanding of what others have said to verify understanding and prevent miscommunication.
- **Written Communication**: The ability to express one's self clearly in business writing.
  - Expresses ideas clearly and concisely in writing.
  - Organizes written ideas clearly and signals the organization to the reader.
  - Tailors written communications to effectively reach an audience.
  - Uses graphics and other aids to clarify complex or technical information.
  - Spells correctly.
  - Writes using concrete, specific language.
  - Uses punctuation correctly.

  - Uses good grammar.
  - Uses an appropriate business writing style.

- **Persuasive Communication**: The ability to plan and deliver oral and written communications that make an impact and persuade their intended audiences.
  - Identifies and presents information or data that will have a strong effect on others.
  - Selects language and examples tailored to the level and experience of the audience.
  - Selects stories, analogies, or examples to illustrate a point.
  - Creates graphics, overheads, or slides that display information clearly and with high impact.
  - Presents several different arguments in support of a position.
- **Interpersonal Awareness**: The ability to notice, interpret, and anticipate others' concerns and feelings, and to communicate this awareness empathetically to others.
  - Understands the interests and important concerns of others.
  - Notices and accurately interprets what others are feeling, based on their choice of words, tone of voice, expressions, and other nonverbal behavior.
  - Anticipates how others will react to a situation.
  - Listens attentively to people's ideas and concerns.
  - Understands both the strengths and the weaknesses of others.
  - Understands the unspoken meaning in a situation.
  - Says or does things to address others' concerns.
  - Finds non-threatening ways to approach others about sensitive issues.
  - Makes others feel comfortable by responding in ways that convey interest in what they have to say.
- **Influencing Others**: The ability to gain others' support for ideas, proposals, projects, and solutions.
  - Presents arguments that address others' most important concerns and issues and looks for win-win solutions.
  - Involves others in a process or decision to ensure their support.
  - Offers trade-offs or exchanges to gain commitment.
  - Identifies and proposes solutions that benefit all parties involved in a situation.
  - Enlists expert or third parties to influence others.

- Develops other indirect strategies to influence others.
- Knows when to escalate critical issues to management, if one's own efforts to enlist support have not succeeded.
- Structures situations to create a desired impact and to maximize the chances of a favorable outcome.
- Works to make a particular impression on others.
- Identifies and targets influence efforts at the real decision makers and those who can influence them.
- Seeks out and builds relationships with others who can provide information, intelligence, career support, potential business, and other forms of help.
- Takes a personal interest in others to develop relationships.
- Accurately anticipates the implications of events or decisions for various stakeholders in the organization and plans strategy accordingly.

▸ **Building Collaborative Relationships**: The ability to develop, maintain, and strengthen partnerships with others inside or outside the organization who can provide information, assistance, and support.

- Asks about the other person's personal experiences, interests, and family.
- Asks questions to identify shared interest, experiences, or other common ground.
- Shows an interest in what others have to say; acknowledges their perspectives and ideas.
- Recognizes the business concerns and perspectives of others.
- Expresses gratitude and appreciation to others who have provided information, assistance, or support.
- Takes time to get to know coworkers, to build rapport and establish a common bond.
- Tries to build relationships with people whose assistance, cooperation, and support may be needed.
- Provides assistance, information, and support to others to build a basis for future reciprocity.

▸ **Customer Orientation**: The ability to demonstrate concern for satisfying one's external and/or internal customers.

- Quickly and effectively solves customer problems.
- Talks to customers to find out what they want and how satisfied they are with what they are getting.

- Lets customers know he is willing to work with them to meet their needs.
- Finds ways to measure and track customer satisfaction.
- Presents a cheerful, positive manner with customers.

II. Competencies Dealing With Business

The Preventing and Solving Problems Cluster

- **Diagnostic Information Gathering**: The ability to identify the information needed to clarify a situation, seek that information from appropriate sources, and use skillful questioning to draw out the information, when others are reluctant to disclose it.
  - Identifies the specific information needed to clarify a situation or to make a decision.
  - Gets more complete and accurate information by checking multiple sources.
  - Probes skillfully to get at the facts, when others are reluctant to provide full, detailed information.
  - Routinely walks around to see how people are doing and to hear about any problems they are encountering.
  - Questions others to assess whether they have thought through a plan of action.
  - Questions others to assess their confidence in solving a problem or tackling a situation.
  - Asks questions to clarify a situation.
  - Seeks the perspective of everyone involved in a situation.
  - Seeks out knowledgeable people to obtain information or clarify a problem.
- **Analytical Thinking**: The ability to tackle a problem by using a logical, systematic, sequential approach.
  - Makes a systematic comparison of two or more alternatives.
  - Notices discrepancies and inconsistencies in available information.
  - Identifies a set of features, parameters or considerations to take into account, in analyzing a situation or making a decision.
  - Approaches a complex task or problem by breaking it down into its component parts and considering each part in detail.
  - Weighs the costs, benefits, risks, and chances for success, in making a decision.

- Identifies many possible causes for a problem.
- Carefully weighs the priority of things to be done.

- **Forward Thinking**: The ability to anticipate the implications and consequences of situations and take appropriate action to be prepared for possible contingencies.
  - Anticipates possible problems and develops contingency plans in advance.
  - Notices trends in the industry or marketplace and develops plans to prepare for opportunities or problems.
  - Anticipates the consequences of situations and plans accordingly.
  - Anticipates how individuals and groups will react to situations and information and plans accordingly.
- **Conceptual Thinking**: The ability to find effective solutions by taking a holistic, abstract, or theoretical perspective.
  - Notices similarities between different and apparently unrelated situations.
  - Quickly identifies the central or underlying issues in a complex situation.
  - Creates a graphic diagram showing a systems view of the situation.
  - Develops analogies or metaphors to explain a situation.
  - Applies a theoretical framework to understand a specific situation.
- **Strategic Thinking**: The ability to analyze the organization's competitive position by considering market and industry trends, existing and potential customers, and strengths and weaknesses as compared to competitors.
  - Understands the organization's strengths and weaknesses as compared to competitors.
  - Understands industry and market trends affecting the organization's competitiveness.
  - Has an in-depth understanding of competitive products and services within the marketplace.
  - Develops and proposes a long-term strategy for the organization based on an analysis of the industry and marketplace and the organization's current and potential capabilities as compared to competitors.

- **Technical Expertise**: The ability to demonstrate depth of knowledge and skill in a technical area.
  - Effectively applies technical knowledge to solve a range of problems.
  - Possesses an in-depth knowledge and skill in a technical area.
  - Develops technical solutions to new or highly complex problems that cannot be solved using existing methods or approaches.
  - Is sought out as an expert to provide advice or solutions in his technical area.
  - Keeps informed about cutting-edge technology in his technical area.

The Achieving Results Cluster

- **Initiative**: Identifying what needs to be done and doing it before being asked or before the situation requires it.
  - Identifying what needs to be done and taking action before being asked or the situation requires it.
  - Does more than what is normally required in a situation.
  - Seeks out others involved in a situation to learn their perspectives.
  - Takes independent action to change the direction of events.
- **Entrepreneurial Orientation**: The ability to look for and seize profitable business opportunities; willingness to take calculated risks to achieve business goals.
  - Notices and seizes profitable business opportunities.
  - Stays abreast of business, industry, and market information that may reveal business opportunities.
  - Demonstrates willingness to take calculated risks to achieve business goals.
  - Proposes innovative business deals to potential customers, suppliers, and business partners.
  - Encourages and supports entrepreneurial behavior in others.
- **Fostering Innovation**: The ability to develop, sponsor, or support the introduction of new and improved methods, products, procedures, or technologies.
  - Personally develops a new product or service.
  - Personally develops a new method or approach.

- Sponsors the development of new products, services, methods or procedures.
- Proposes new approaches, methods or technologies.
- Develops better, faster or less expensive ways to do things.
- Works cooperatively with others to produce innovative solutions.

- **Results Orientation**: The ability to focus on the desired result of one's own or one's unit's work, setting challenging goals. Focusing effort on the goals, and meeting or exceeding them.
  - Develops challenging but achievable goals.
  - Develops clear goals for meetings and projects.
  - Maintains commitment to goals in the face of obstacle and frustration.
  - Finds or creates ways to measure performance against goals.
  - Exerts unusual effort over time to achieve a goal.
  - Has a strong sense of urgency about solving problems and getting work done.
- **Thoroughness**: Ensuring that one's own work and information are complete and accurate; carefully preparing for meetings and presentations; following up with others to ensure that agreements and commitments have been fulfilled.
  - Sets up procedures to ensure high quality of work.
  - Monitors the quality of work.
  - Verifies information.
  - Checks the accuracy of own and others work.
  - Develops and uses systems to organize and keep track of information or work progress.
  - Carefully prepares for meetings and presentations.
  - Organizes information or material for others.
  - Carefully review and checks the accuracy of information in work reports provided by management, IT, or other individuals and groups.
- **Decisiveness**: The ability to make decisions in a timely manner.
  - Is willing to make decisions in difficult or ambiguous situations, when time is critical.
  - Takes charge of a group when it is necessary to facilitate change, overcome an impasse, face issues, or ensure decisions are made.
  - Makes tough decisions.

III. Self-Management Competencies

- **Self Confidence**: Faith in one's own ideas and capability to be successful; willingness to take an independent position in the face of opposition.
  - Is confident of own ability to accomplish goals.
  - Presents self crisply and impressively.
  - Is willing to speak up to the right person or group at the right time, when he disagrees with a decision or strategy.
  - Approaches challenging tasks with a "can-do" attitude.
- **Stress Management**: The ability to keep functioning effectively when under pressure and maintain self control in the face of hostility or provocation.
  - Remains calm under stress.
  - Can effectively handle several problems or tasks at once.
  - Controls his response when criticized, attacked, or provoked.
  - Maintains a sense of humor under difficult circumstances.
  - Manages own behavior to prevent or reduce feelings of stress.
- **Personal Credibility**: Demonstrated concern that one be perceived as responsible, reliable, and trustworthy.
  - Does what he commits to doing.
  - Respects the confidentiality of information or concerns shared by others.
  - Is honest and forthright with people.
  - Carries his fair share of the workload.
  - Takes responsibility for own mistakes; does not blame others.
  - Conveys a command of the relevant facts and information.
- **Flexibility:** Openness to different and new ways of doing things; willingness to modify one's preferred way of doing things.
  - Is able to see the merits of perspectives other than his own.
  - Demonstrates openness to new organizational structures, procedures, and technology.
  - Switches to a different strategy when an initially selected one is unsuccessful.
  - Demonstrates willingness to modify a strongly held position in the face of contrary evidence.

Appendix B

Competencies for Case Studies

Corporate Attorney Key Competencies:

- Achieves Results.
- Impact and Influence.
- Customer Service.
- Analytical Skills.
- Strategic Agility.
- Team Orientation.

Questions:

1. Tell me about a time when you used your judgment to persuade a partner or senior manager to make a different decision in a case.
   - Impact and Influence.
   - Customer Service.
   - Team Orientation.
   - Achieves Results.
2. Tell me about a time when you used complex litigation analysis in a case. What was the result?
   - Achieves Results.
   - Analytical Skills.
3. Have you used a litigation strategy? Describe a case where you used a litigation strategy to help you manage the case, and tell us the steps you went through to determine the right litigation strategy to use. What happened?

- Strategic Agility.
- Analytical Skills.
- Achieves Results.

4. Tell us about a time when you had to deal with a difficult issue with an employee. How did you handle it? What happened?
   - Customer Service.
   - Impact and Influence.
   - Team Orientation.
5. Describe a situation in which you had to deal with a difficult client. How did you handle the situation?
   - Customer Service.
   - Impact and Influence.
   - Team Orientation.
   - Strategic Agility.
6. Tell us about a time when you used your skills and knowledge to help the team. What was your role? What was the outcome or result of your input?
   - Team Orientation.
   - Impact and Influence.
   - Achieves Results.

Human Resources Vice President Key Competencies:

- Achieves Results.
- Impact and Influence.
- Customer Focus.
- Building Business Partnerships, Relationships, and Teams.
- Consulting.
- Organizational Awareness, Agility, and Savvy.
- Providing Feedback.
- Understanding Business Goals.
- Human Resources Expertise.

Questions

1. Describe a time when you had to work especially hard to get a good result. What did you do?
   - Achieves Results.
   - Understanding Business Goals.
   - Impact and Influence.
   - Organizational Awareness, Agility, and Savvy.
2. Tell us about a time when you had to influence a group of people to be able to lead them effectively.
   - Impact and Influence.
   - Building Business Partnerships, Relationships, and Teams.
   - Customer Focus.
   - Achieves Results.
   - Organizational Awareness, Agility, and Savvy.
   - Providing Feedback.
3. When you first started with your current employer, what did you do to learn the specific things about the industry that you needed to know to be effective in human resources? How did you decide what was especially important?
   - Understanding Business Goals.
   - Customer Focus.
   - Human Resources Expertise.
   - Consulting.
4. Tell us about one of the most effective business partnerships you've been involved in building. What did you do to help make it so effective? Did you have to overcome any obstacles? Describe what happened.
   - Building Business Partnerships, Relationships, and Teams.
   - Achieves Results.
   - Organizational Awareness, Agility, and Savvy.
   - Impact and Influence.
   - Customer Focus.
   - Providing Feedback.

5. Have you been involved with introducing any new ideas or programs into your organization? Tell us about the program, and describe the steps you used to improve the acceptance for the program.
   - Understanding Business Goals.
   - Human Resources Expertise.
   - Achieves Results.
   - Impact and Influence.
   - Customer Focus.
   - Building Business Partnerships, Relationships, and Teams.
   - Consulting.
   - Organizational Awareness, Agility, and Savvy.
   - Providing Feedback.
6. Tell us about a time when you made a mistake. What did you learn from it?
   - Customer Focus.
   - Building Business Partnerships, Relationships, and Teams.
   - Consulting.
   - Organizational Awareness, Agility, and Savvy.
   - Impact and Influence.

Director, Information Technology
Key Competencies:

- Creates Innovative Solutions.
- Thinks Analytically.
- Acts Strategically and Globally.
- Drives Results.
- Exceeds Customer Expectations.
- Risk-Taking.
- Acts Decisively.
- Collaborates and Influences Others.
- Demonstrates Integrity.
- Treats People with Respect.
- Manages Performance.
- Develops People.
- Manages Change.

Questions:

1. Tell us about a situation in which you had to take several actions over a period of time and overcome obstacles in order to achieve a business objective.
   - Drives Results.
   - Thinks Analytically.
   - Manages Performance.
   - Acts Strategically and Globally.
2. Describe a time when you had to identify some key issues in order to guide a group toward the right decision.
   - Collaborates and Influences Others.
   - Thinks Analytically.
   - Acts Strategically and Globally.
   - Drives Results.
   - Acts Decisively.
   - Demonstrates Integrity.
   - Treats People with Respect.
   - Manages Performance.
   - Develops People.
3. Think of a time when you had many challenging projects with different priorities to manage. Tell us about it.
   - Drives Results.
   - Creates Innovative Solutions.
   - Thinks Analytically.
   - Acts Strategically and Globally.
   - Exceeds Customer Expectations.
   - Risk-Taking.
   - Acts Decisively.
   - Collaborates and Influences Others.
   - Demonstrates Integrity.
   - Treats People with Respect.
   - Manages Performance.
   - Develops People.
   - Manages Change.

College Graduate, Engineering
Key Competencies:

- Achieved Results.
- Initiative.
- Analytical Skills.
- Customer Service.
- Engineering and Computer Competencies.
- Planning and Organizing.
- Information Seeking.

Questions:

1. Tell me about an assignment in school or at work that required strong analytical skills. How did you plan and organize the work? How did you decide what information you would need?
   - Analytical Skills.
   - Planning and Organizing.
   - Information Seeking.
   - Initiative.
   - Achieved Results.
   - Technical Competencies.
2. Have you worked with a difficult customer? Describe what happened.
   - Customer Service.
   - Information Seeking.
   - Initiative.
3. Tell me about the most difficult engineering or computer project you've worked on. Describe what obstacles you ran into, and tell me how you overcame them.
   - Achieved Results.
   - Initiative.
   - Analytical Skills.
   - Engineering and Computer Competencies.
   - Planning and Organizing.
   - Information Seeking.

Appendix C

Examples of Illegal Interview Questions

1. What is your country of citizenship?
2. When were you born?
3. Where do you go to church?
4. What is your native language?
5. Where were your parents born?
6. Are you married?
7. Do you have or plan on having children?
8. What are your childcare arrangements?
9. Are you gay or straight?
10. Do you have any disabilities?
11. Have you had any recent illness or operations?
12. What type of military discharge did you obtain?
13. Tell me about your family.
14. When did you graduate from high school?

Notes

Chapter 1

1. Lou Adler, "The Best Interview Question of All Time." *www.erexchange.com*, June 28, 2001.

Chapter 2

1. *www.ohr.psu.edu/competencies/ohr/Employee%20handbook%20final.pdf.*
2. Adapted from Robert Wood and Tim Payne, *Competency-Based Recruitment and Selection* (Chichester, UK: John Wiley & Sons, 1998), 28.

Chapter 3

1. Source for statistic: *www.eeoc.gov/stats/charges.html.*

Chapter 6

1. The last seven tips on this list are adapted from Joseph A. DeVito, *Human Communication: The Basic Course*, Fifth Edition (HarperCollins Publishers, 1991), 153.

Chapter 7

1. Robin Kessler and Linda A. Strasburg. *Competency-Based Resumes: How to Bring Your Resume to the Top of the Pile* (Franklin Lakes, NJ: Career Press, 2004), 175–177.

Chapter 8

1. Robin Kessler and Linda A. Strasburg. *Competency-Based Resumes: How to Bring Your Resume to the Top of the Pile* (Franklin Lakes, NJ: Career Press, 2004), 38.

Chapter 11

1. Source: *http://www.brainyquote.com/quotes/quotes/a/arthurccl101182.html#ixzz1n9QiEMrL*.
2. Source: Wikipedia.com.

Chapter 12

1. Source: *http://en.wikipedia.org/wiki/Northwestern_University_in_Qatar.*
2. "Defining the Content Domain of Intercultural Competence for Global Leaders." Allan Bird, Mark Mendenhall, Michael J. Stevens, Gary Oddou. *Journal of Managerial Psychology*, Volume 25, No. 8, 2010, p. 811.
3. Ibid, p. 814.
4. Adapted from Ibid, p. 815–820.
5. Ibid, p. 816.
6. Ibid, p. 815.
7. From: *http://en.wikipedia.org/wiki/Public_Service_Commission_of_Canada#Public_Service_Employment_Act.*
8. Ibid.
9. From: *http://www.cra-arc.gc.ca/crrs/wrkng/ssssmnt/cmptncy2008/menu-eng.html.*
10. From: *http://www.cra-arc.gc.ca/crrs/wrkng/ssssmnt/bhvrlntrvw/trgtd_bhvrl_ntrvw_nstrctns-eng.html.*
11. Ibid.
12. Statistics on India from Wikipedia.com.
13. From "The Indian CEO: A Portrait of Excellence" (white paper, Hay Group Website: *http://www.haygroup.com/downloads/ww/indian_ceo_for_web2.pdf*).
14. Ibid.
15. Ibid.

Bibliography

Adler, Lou. *Hire With Your Head: Using Power Hiring to Build Great Companies*, Second Edition. Hoboken, N.J.: John Wiley & Sons, Inc., 2002.

Adler, Ronald B., and Jeanne Marquardt Elmhorst. *Communicating at Work: Principles and Practices for Business and the Professions*, 8th edition. Boston: McGraw Hill, 2004.

Boyatzis, Richard. *The Competent Manager: A Model for Effective Performance*. New York: John Wiley and Sons, 1982.

Cooper, Kenneth Carlton. *Effective Competency Modeling and Reporting: A Step-by-Step Guide for Improving Individual & Organizational Performance.* New York: Amacom, 2000.

Cripe, Edward J., and Richard S. Mansfield. *The Value-Added Employee*. Woodburn, Mass.: Butterworth-Heinemann, 2002.

DeVito, Joseph. *Human Communication: The Basic Course*, 9th edition. Boston: Allyn & Bacon, 2002.

Dobkin, Bethami, and Roger C. Pace. *Communication in a Changing World*. Boston: McGraw Hill, 2003.

Fry, Ron. *101 Great Answers to the Toughest Interview Questions*, Third Edition. Franklin Lakes, N.J.: Career Press, 1996.

Green, Paul C. *Building Robust Competencies: Linking Human Resources Systems to Organizational Strategies.* San Francisco, Calif.: Jossey-Bass, 1999.

Kessler, Robin, and Linda A. Strasburg. *Competency-Based Resumes: How to Bring Your Resume to the Top of the Pile*. Franklin Lakes, N.J.: Career Press, 2004.

Lombardo, Michael M., and Robert W. Eichinger. *The Leadership Machine: Architecture to Develop Leaders for Any Future*. Minneapolis: Lominger, 2001.

Powers, Dr. Paul. *Winning Job Interviews: Reduce Interview Anxiety, Outprepare the Other Candidates, Land the Job You Love*. Franklin Lakes, N.J.: Career Press, 2004.

Quinn, Carol. *Don't Hire Anyone Without Me!: A Revolutionary Approach to Interviewing & Hiring the Best*. Franklin Lakes, N.J.: Career Press, 2001.

Spencer, Jr., Lyle M., PhD, and Signe M. Spencer. *Competence at Work: Models for Superior Performance*. New York: John Wiley & Sons, Inc., 1993.

Wendleton, Kate. *Interviewing and Salary Negotiation*. Clifton Park, N.Y.: Thomson Delmar Learning, 1999.

——. *Mastering the Job Interview and Winning the Money Game*. Clifton Park, N.Y.: Thomson Delmar Learning, 2005.

Wood, Robert, and Tim Payne. *Competency-Based Recruitment and Selection: A Practical Guide*. Chichester, England: John Wiley & Sons, 2003.

Yates, Martin. *Knock 'Em Dead 2005: The Ultimate Job Seekers Guide*. Avon, Mass.: Adams Media Corporation, 2004.

Index

A

accomplishment statements, 172-173
accomplishments, current list of your, 175
Achievement/Results Oriented, 72-73, 75
action, 47, 54, 55, 61, 62, 63, 64
    Integrity and Credo-Based, 45, 46
active language, 126
Adler, Lou, 21
analytical skills, 82
answers, giving good, 64-65
approach, most typical, 22
approaches, understand competency-based interview, 89
articulate, are you, 42
assessment centers, 141-142
attire, 69, 72
avoiding
    legal problems, 43-45
    potential problems, 65-66

B

Baby Boomers, 138, 140
behavioral questions, competency-based, 52-53
Berra, Yogi, 41
body of interview, 116

C

Canada, 156-157
candidate, presenting yourself as a strong, 69-78
career, actively managing your, 171-177
case studies, 101-113
case study interview questions, answering, 143-145
centers, assessment, 141-142
changes, technology, 145
coaching, 117-119, 124-136
communication and technology, 142-143
communication, nonverbal, 69-71, 96-97

competence, proving your own, 53
competencies,
 10 most common, 35
 developing, 174
 proving, 59-68
competency gaps, 83
competency list, identify the right, 90
competency-based interviews, definition, 13
competency-based interview systems, understanding, 19-27
conclusion of interview, 119-121
core competencies, list of, 193-204
corporate culture and competencies, 45
Credo-Based Actions, Integrity and, 45
critical competencies, selecting, 37
customer service, 60, 64, 75

D

developing critical competencies, 174
dressing appropriately, 43
Driven, Results and Performance, 23, 45
Drucker, Peter, 51

E

education, 184
EEO, 44
employer and the interviewer, understand the needs of the, 91-92
Equal Employment Opportunity, 44, *see also* EEO
Ethics and Integrity, 60, 64
eye contact, 69, 72

F

Facebook, 138
FEMA, 35
fit, 42
flexibility,
 interest, 155
 social, 155
flow of a competency-based interview, 115-121
follow up, 163-170
future, global competencies for the, 151-161

G

gaps,
 competency, 83
 overcoming competency, 174
general competencies, 30
gestures, 69
global competencies for the future, develop, 151-161
global leadership profile, 33
Google, 139
grammar, 42

H

humor, sense of, 43

I

illegal questions, 43
Impact and Influence, 75

India, 157-159
individual competency, 15
initiative, 53-57, 64
Integrity and Credo-Based Actions, 45, 46
Integrity and Ethics, 60-62, 74-75
intercultural competencies, 153-155
interest flexibility, 155
internet, social media and the, 138-139
Interpersonal Understanding, 158
interview systems, understanding competency-based, 19-27
interview,
 flow of a competency-based, 115-121
 getting your next, 179-188
interviewees, learn from, 123-136
interviewers
 and what they have always been looking for, 42-43
 are trained to look for, know what, 41-49
interviews,
 comparing the two types of, 25-26
 videoconference, 141
 what are competency-based, 13
introduction of interview, 115-116

J

job postings on competitors' Websites, look at, 31
job, can you do the, 42

K

Key Points, 38-39, 48, 57-58, 67-68, 76-78, 86-88, 146-150, 159-161, 169-170, 186-188

L

language,
 active, 126
 positive, 57
leadership attributes, Boeing, 30
learn from interviewees, 123-136
legal problems, how are interviewers taught to avoid, 43-45
levels, three to five competency, 36
LinkedIn, 138
look for, know what interviewers are trained to, 41-49
looking for, what have interviewers always been, 42-43
Lord of the Rings, 69

M

management, perception, 155
managing your career, actively, 171-177
Mid-Book Review, 89-99
modesty, 60

N

negotiate, 163-170
Newton, Sir Isaac, 101
nonjudgementalness, 155
nonverbal communication, 69-71, 71-75, 96-97

nonverbal tips, 76
note, thank-you, 165-166

O

obvious competencies for the position, think about, 31
offer, get the, 163-170
Onassiss, Aristotle, 41
The One Question Interview, 21
organizations that match your values, focus on, 64
organized answers, 70
Organizing, Planning and, 36
Orientation, Achievement/Results, 72-73

P

PAR, 47
perception management, 155
performance appraisals, 172-173
Performance Driven, Results and, 45
personality, 43
Planning and Organizing, 36
plans, employee development, 172-173
position, list the competencies for your, 31
positive language, 57
practice, 51
practices, stay current with interview technology and, 137-150
preparing for interview questions, 53
problems, avoiding potential, 65-66
Proust, Marcel, 189-192
proving competencies, 59-68

Q

questionnaire, interview, 83-85
questions,
    competency-based behavioral, 52-53
    prepare to answer competency based interview, 93-95
    preparing for behavioral, 53

R

ranking competencies, 47
RATS, 47
responding to behavioral questions, 52
result, 47, 54, 55, 61, 62, 63, 64
Results and Performance Driven, 45
Results, Achieves, 124
resume,
    competency-based, 179-185
    yelling on your, 185
Review, Mid-Book, 89-99

S

salary, 81-82
selecting critical competencies, 37
situation, 61, 62, 64,
situation/problem, 54, 55
situation/task, 47
skills,
    analytical, 82
    good social, 42
    technical, 184
Skype and Webcams, 140-141
smiling, 70
social flexibility, 155
social media and the internet, 138-139
space, personal, 70

STAR, 47, 125
statements, accomplishment, 172-173
steps to writing a thank-you note, 165-166
strengths, what are your, 82
studies, case, 101-113

T

task, 47
technology changes, 145
technology, stay current with interview practices and, 137-150
thank-you notes, 163-170
Thatcher, Margaret, 171
tips,
    nonverbal, 76
    other important, 79-88
tone, 65
track your competencies, systems to, 173
train for competency-based interviews, interviewers and how they, 45-47

U

Understanding, Interpersonal, 158

V

values, focus on organizations that match your, 64
videoconference interviews, 141
virtual assessment centers, 141-142
virtue, modesty is never a, 60

W

weakness, what is your greatest, 82-83
Webcams and Skype, 140-141
win, what it takes to, 9

About the Author

Robin Kessler is president of The Interview Coach, a human resources and career consulting firm based in Houston, Texas. She teaches classes in business and professional communication, interviewing, management, and leadership as an adjunct professor for the University of Houston–Downtown. Robin has more than 20 years of experience improving interviews, resumes, presentations, and organization communication as a human resources professional, consultant, and career coach. She is also the author of *Competency-Based Performance Reviews* and *Competency-Based Resumes*, both published by Career Press. She has written articles on current issues in organization communication and speaking skills for publications including *HR Magazine*, *Employment Relations Today*, and the *Houston Chronicle*; has been a guest speaker at conferences; and has been interviewed for newspapers, magazines, and radio and television programs. Robin received her BA and MBA from Northwestern University. Please contact her with your comments at intvcoach@aol.com or connect with her on LinkedIn.